Margaret Helfand Architects

Margaret Helfand Architects

Essential Architecture

Introduction by Paola Antonelli

Photographs by Paul Warchol

Text by Margaret Helfand

THE MONACELLI PRESS

for Phyllis, Bunny, and Jon

First published in the United States
of America in 1999 by
The Monacelli Press, Inc.
10 East 92nd Street
New York, New York 10128

Library of Congress
Cataloging-in-Publication Data
Helfand, Margaret.
Margaret Helfand Architects : essential
architecture / introduction by Paola
Antonelli ; photographs by Paul Warchol ;
text by Margaret Helfand.
p.   cm.—(Work in progress)
Includes bibliographical references.
ISBN 1-885254-93-8
1. Margaret Helfand Architects. 2. Archi-
tecture, Modern—20th century—United
States. I. Antonelli, Paola, 1963– .
II. Title. III. Series: Work in progress
(New York, N.Y.).
NA737.M2166H45   1998
720'.92'2—dc21   98-40927

Printed in Hong Kong

Designed by Paul Montie, Fahrenheit
with assistance from Josh Silverman

Cover: Cloister for Learning,
photograph by Timothy Hursley

All photographs by Paul Warchol,
with the exception of:
pages 139–55, 166–67,
photographs by Timothy Hursley

Contents

Modern Realism

Paola Antonelli

Margaret Helfand's work embodies the unique character of contemporary American modern architecture. Such work might be considered a blending of inspirations, or a consequence of brewing the melting pot, but Helfand refers to it as a "process of distillation." What she has distilled, that is, what is common to all of her projects, is the sense of economy and sensibility that distinguishes the American brand of modern from that of any other country.

In the Western world, the rules and regulations of the modern movement have become the point of reference for all architecture, both conceived and produced. While a modern attitude, identified by the search for an objective approach to designing and building, has forever existed, its formalist codification in the course of the twentieth century has elevated it to a pervasive moral and aesthetic principle.

In each nation and in each decade, the modern has taken on different nuances, susceptible as it is to artistic trends as well as to sociopolitical developments. In the United States, as Kenneth Frampton has written, "The 'movement' had . . . to be more sensitive to the issue of popular acceptance and to this end its anti-monumentality stemmed directly from its use of native materials and from its response to the vagaries of topography and climate."[1]

As is customary with American cultural currents, modern architecture presented slightly different personalities on the East and West coasts. The East Coast architectural aristocracy, led by the Museum of Modern Art and Harvard University, had in the 1930s invited and embraced the mighty vision of émigrés Walter Gropius and Ludwig Mies van der Rohe. Gropius had come to the edge of the Atlantic, to Harvard's Graduate School of Design, in 1937, and there taught Edward Larrabee Barnes, Philip Johnson, I. M. Pei, and Paul Rudolph, among others. On the West Coast, however, the legacy of the New Deal lingered on, even after 1945. While Eastern architects were more keen on translating the word of the modern movement into public buildings and gemlike private residences for the upper classes, Western architects were dealing with everyday life in a discrete, ad hoc fashion. Likewise, while the trademark European modernism of the 1930s relied heavily on ideology, West Coast modern, based as it was on a straightforward and optimistic realism, was the champion of an American sensibility and idealism.

The new architecture "for modern living"[2] established itself after World War II as an innovative way to represent and accommodate the booming middle class, all the while using materials and techniques made available by the idle war industries. It was about practice, not theory, and It required that homes be comfortable and efficient, both in the way they were used and in the way they were built. Unusually, since the new archi tecture was aimed at the home, its guidelines were forged by the domestic sensibility of its main inhabitants, women.

California modern thrived, not only because of the state's natural and sociological settings, but also because many factories were located there. The Case Study Houses program, directed in the Los Angeles area by John Entenza through his *Arts and Architecture* magazine, can be hailed as its manifesto. Between 1945 and 1966, thirty-six prototypes of modern family houses were proposed by some of the best architects on the West Coast, and many of them were actually built. They all exemplified the clean, well-lighted ideal place that the healthy Californian middle class longed for.

American modern, because of its pragmatic, rather than ideological, basis and its practical concerns, was allowed a delightful freedom that in European circles would have been considered heresy. Suzanne Stephens summarized the formal principles of American modern—on both coasts—as they developed after World War II: "A strong value [was] placed on simple, functional planning, the straightforward expression of structure, and the integration of indoor with outdoor spaces. It also meant the employment of the latest technologies in building construction. Applied ornament was naturally eschewed, since beauty was a by-product resulting from good planning and logical building."[3] Since no code was ever written, the following decades saw more crossovers between material and popular culture, such as the use of local mate- rials instead of steel and glass. An example is Sea Ranch, the compound designed in 1964 by MLTW (Moore Lyndon Turnbull Whitaker) Associates. Built with local wood and laid out to respect and enhance the natural setting of the Northern California coast, Sea Ranch could hardly be recognized as "modern" according to conventional wisdom. Nevertheless, this kind of modern architecture allowed Ameri- can architects finally to find their local culture and their historical context, for which they had long envied Europe.

In the 1960s and 1970s, while many architects in the Old World, like Archigram or Günther Domenig, were openly confronting the modern movement, which they con- sidered obsolete, in an attempt to rebel against its *diktat* and update architecture to a new world order, American modernism continued undisturbed, seamlessly absorb- ing the political and economic turmoil. In the 1970s, the oil crisis and public aware- ness of environmental problems inflected modern architecture toward "indigenous construction methods, conserving energy use, and preserving old structures."[4] Incidentally, that time saw the first formulation of a feminist critique of architecture and design.

Helfand matured as an architect at the exact time when, curiously enough, much American modern, on both coasts, had become a unique form of simplified vernacu- lar architecture. This formulation allowed her to blend many experiences and references into one single expression. As a matter of fact, Helfand's own brand of modern presents even more interesting influences from empirical research or, quite simply, from living intensely.

Margaret Helfand grew up in Los Angeles and often visited Mexico when still a child. Aztec and Mayan monuments were her first contacts with the magnitude and brilliance of indigenous architecture. A mere six years old when she first traveled to Europe, she remembers the impression that medieval architecture had on her. "The freshness and directness of early modern looks as timeless to me today as medieval architecture and 'primitive' architecture . . . Is it possible that in the twenty-first century we have to do less to move forward?" she asks. To this day, she cherishes her copy of *Architecture Without Architects*, the fundamental exhibition catalog by Bernard Rudofsky that marked the time that this kind of architecture—"we shall call it vernacular, anonymous, spontaneous, indigenous, rural, as the case may be"[5]— invaded the Museum of Modern Art. Her second trip to Europe, as a teenager, included Scandinavia and provided her with her first experience of full-fledged modernism.

Helfand attended Swarthmore College in Pennsylvania, where she studied art history and was first exposed to Pennsylvania Quaker culture; in the late 1960s she enrolled in the College of Environmental Design at the University of California at Berkeley. Architecture school was not a formative experience in her life. The school was often on strike, the price one had to pay to be at the very center of the counterculture in the 1960s. In Berkeley, the agenda was political rather than artistic. Helfand had purposely chosen not to go to a conservative East Coast school and admits having selected Berkeley because it had a lively intellectual life. While in school, she went to work for Backen, Arrigoni & Ross in San Francisco, which turned out to be her first real education in architecture.

In 1970, Helfand temporarily left the school before graduating, traveled to Europe, and together with nineteen friends bought a ninety-foot three-masted wooden schooner in Sweden for $7,000. Happily set in a communal way of life, they sailed to Spain and started to rebuild the boat. Helfand lived on board and finally learned how to build things. Using the wood shop they built on the boat, she became a skilled cabinetmaker and learned a great deal about heavy carpentry and construction. She was also in charge of working the braided wire cable to make standing rigging for the masts and learned welding and grinding steel to help make water tanks and spars. She acquired at that time a deep respect for materials and craftsmanship. From Spain, the schooner sailed through the Mediterranean, to the Cape Verde Islands, and then on to the Caribbean. When the group ran out of money, they carried cargo out of Trinidad to the islands.

After two years, she took a hiatus from sailing and returned to Berkeley to complete her master's degree. Shortly thereafter, she was back on the schooner and ready to sail for another year from Costa Rica across the South Pacific. Her confidence in construction solidified and her horizons expanded to include many discoveries of local materials, cultures, and construction techniques. In Tonga and Samoa, she was struck by the buildings made of coconut palm trunks and woven palm leaves. The classic Samoan house was beautiful, modern, minimal, and pure, while at the same time natural, biodegradable, and environmentally correct—all in all, a timeless modern ideal. The photographs Helfand took twenty-five years ago are to this day an inspiration and a reminder that architecture is about achieving the best results while doing what is deemed possible; that architecture is about economy of thought, design, and construction.

Back from the Pacific, Helfand moved to New York, still working with Backen, Arrigoni & Ross, on a project in Iran. While in the city, she heard that Marcel Breuer, whose office was in the 1970s still a cathedral devoted to pure modernism, was looking for help on a charrette in the Middle East. She went to work for his firm on that temporary basis and was then offered a position. She stayed for five years, from 1976 to 1981, and she was the first woman in the office to become an associate in architecture.

Not only was Breuer one of Helfand's idols, but he also cherished her favorite parts of the architectural process: materials and building techniques. He used to ask his collaborators for full-size prototypes of architectural details made of the actual materials to test the construction process of any single building. Helfand thus had a chance to refine both her passion for the modern and her knowledge of its materials and techniques.

In 1981, she started her own practice, Margaret Helfand Architects. Since then, the office has produced a very wide variety of commercial, institutional, and residential projects, all infused by the same sense of economy and simplicity, and by an urgency made necessary by the evolution of society. Helfand, forever the aware and eager 1960s youth, declares that "because our life experience is becoming increasingly complex, with global travel and communications, and because our population on this planet is growing exponentially, we have a responsibility to minimize the complexity of our man-made environment and create simple, functional, timeless solutions in architecture as well as in other areas of production." Helfand, honestly addressing the signs of the times, demonstrates an undeniably modern attitude.

"My desire is to seek simplification, to seek the essence of things. My work—and that of my colleagues at the office—has discarded all preconceived architectural ideas except, perhaps, Vitruvius's dictum that architecture should encompass 'firmness, commodity, and delight,' and the idea that there is delight in accomplishing 'firmness and commodity' with the least complex means, rather in the same manner that the shortest and simplest solution to a mathematical problem is considered the most 'elegant' (and therefore the best) by mathematicians." While time and budget constraints often become the most interesting challenges, Helfand's obsessive quest for simplification comes from many different sources, which range from her Californian and American sense of moral responsibility to her passion for the minimalism of Donald Judd, Sol Lewitt, Richard Serra, Michael Heizer, and all the artists she became exposed to when she moved to New York.

Like appropriate materials and forms, a minimalism that is all about careless elegance is a deeply American attitude. In 1996, Margaret Helfand Architects designed and built the new Kohlberg Hall for Swarthmore College in Pennsylvania (Cloister for Learning). The beautiful building, made of indigenous stone, belongs so naturally to its context that it looks many decades old. It is dated to the 1990s only by the dichroic glass extensively used for exterior glazing and its contemporary simplified lines. In a

Travel Snapshots, 1990s

Street, Tripotomos,
Tínos, Greece, 1993

Chapel, San Galgano,
Italy, 1997

Fortress of Sacsayhuaman,
Cuzco, Peru, 1996

critique of the project, Thomas Hine referred to the Quaker idea of plainness, as opposed to the "obsessively refined simplicity of the Shakers." He declares that such a "Quaker ideal of plainness has produced, more often than not, buildings of time-less awkwardness that fuse the durable and the dowdy."[6] Helfand has a slightly different conception of the essence of Quaker: sobriety.

"I believe that people love our work because there is no excess. Everything has a purpose. Nonetheless, there is coherence and a philosophical position," Helfand explains. A recognition in her work of the strong moral sense of the oldest Protestant communities makes Helfand proud. In that ethical tradition are the very roots of minimalism. Helfand embraces this very modern ethos, in the belief "that architecture can spring directly from the process by which it is made, with a minimum of elaboration . . . [Its] components are in turn made of materials that have their own logic of form, which is based on their nature or the fabrication process." This statement, which was formulated in 1998 but might as well be excerpted from a protomodernist text written at the beginning of the century, exemplifies the new age of modernism worldwide. It unites Helfand with the group of architects, like Peter Zumthor in Switzerland and Alvaro Siza in Portugal and Spain, who are keeping alive the old flame of the "truth of materials."

Helfand's use of materials is based on empirical knowledge. Upon meeting each one of them, be it steel, granite, or the parallel strand lumber she recently used to define the interior structure of a workplace in New York (Temporary Workplace), she sets out to see what it can do by bending, folding, or cutting it diagonally. The meeting room in the Helfand office is adorned with a long table and chairs obtained by cutting and bending a steel plate in a geometric series (Workspace for Architects; X, Y, Z, W Chairs).

In a similar fashion, Helfand readily devotes attention to a new technology, when it proves to be appropriate to the project, another quality placing her squarely in the tradition of American modernism. In what can be considered one of her most reve-latory projects, the 1993 Child Development Center for Bronx Community College (Preassembled School), budget problems led Helfand to adapt the plan into a mod-ular one. This change was in response to a suggestion by the CDC director, who had heard of "an innovative construction/financing strategy: factory-built buildings, avail-able on lease-purchase."[7] The size of the classrooms for preschool children and training of educators on the lower level has defined the whole project, with no loss of architectural expression. Logical beauty, the successful outcome to a constrained situation, is the goal of Margaret Helfand Architects.

Helfand brings the same kind of exploration and articulation to the architectural plan. Her architecture often displays many moving parts, sometimes whole portions of walls, as portrayed by her 1998 Workspace for Film Production. Parts, materials, and spaces depend on each other in an attempt to achieve a fluid coherence among the various scales and enhance the dynamic quality of the space. "People always respond well to gestures and end up using the spaces with the same continuity of movement," she says. The kinetic quality of her architecture results from her long years of train-ing with Merce Cunningham and Erick Hawkins. A particularly emblematic project, one that unfortunately did not get built, is the 1996 design for Lt. Petrosino Park (Urban Park), a difficult residual triangle in New York's Soho defined by the crossing of three streets and a below-ground subway station. The subtle and fascinating proposal is almost nothing but articulated movement, the same "dynamism plus efficiency" that guided Buckminster Fuller's Dymaxion House since its first version in 1927.

Helfand calls her architecture a "process of distillation." "You have needs, therefore you build, and you build using materials. We try to solve each design problem like a mathematical formula, with an economy of means and an elegance in the relationship of the parts." And since she declares that, given the nature of what she does, she will never be a theoretical architect, in this book she sets out to give a precise and minimalist description of her firm's work in a rigorously logical scheme. She adopts matter-of-fact language and proceeds with adamant, almost defiant simplicity in an elaboration by axiom. The format is based on what she has recognized as her own three lines of thought: geometry, or what gives architecture its inner order and form; structure, the composition that sets architecture in relation to the context and to its users; and materials, which give architecture its soul. She calls these three lines of thought "axes."

Helfand's introductory statement may provide the last overt sense of the individuality of the architect. The discussions of each project are clear-cut and analytical, rather than narrative; the process is the subject. In fact, the search for clarity and objectivity so fundamental to the modern faith requires that architects take a backseat. Interestingly enough, the projects almost seem to have self-generated out of necessity, possibly by parthenogenesis. The contemporary American modern realist attitude also entails combining in time and space to best represent the spirit of the moment. In her own process of distillation, Helfand has elevated personal history, architectural history, gender, and social concerns to their just universal sphere, in which architects are the interpreters between what architecture wants and what architecture can be.

1. Kenneth Frampton, "The Eclipse of the New Deal: Buckminster Fuller, Philip Johnson and Louis Kahn 1934–64," *Modern Architecture: A Critical History* (New York: Oxford University Press, 1980), 239.

2. *Blueprints for Modern Living: History and Legacy of the Case Study Houses* is the title of an exhibition and catalog curated by Elizabeth A. T. Smith at the Museum of Contemporary Art, Los Angeles, 1989.

3. Suzanne Stephens, "The 1970s: A Time of Upheaval," in *Modern American Houses*, ed. Clifford A. Pearson (New York: Harry N. Abrams/Architectural Record, 1996), 103.

4. Stephens, "The 1970s," 103.

5. Bernard Rudofsky, preface to *Architecture Without Architects* (New York: Museum of Modern Art, 1964).

6. Thomas Hine, "Analysis: Margaret Helfand's Kohlberg Hall at Swarthmore College Is Quaker in Substance, not in Style," *Architectural Record*, February 1997, 71.

7. Ziva Freiman, "Joint Effort," *Progressive Architecture,* March 1995, 56–63.

This Book

Margaret Helfand

This book is about why we do what we do.

These twenty projects are laboratory experiments conducted over the last ten years to investigate a hypothesis: that architecture can spring directly from the process by which it is made, with a minimum of elaboration.

This making consists of three elements:

geometry

> Any design solution must begin with a commitment to some form of order. Architects have historically used geometries based on stylistic precepts, such as axial ordering in classical Greek architecture or asymmetry in modernism. But other ordering systems are possible. The projects in this book demonstrate architecture that results from geometries based on program (Industrial Building), circulation (Workspace for Architects), and context (Vertical House on a Trapezoidal Site).

> The second role of geometry is in giving form. Buildings, building components, and functional elements within buildings all have form. These components are in turn made of materials that have their own logic of form, which is based on their nature or the fabrication process. Metal is usually configured into flat, rectangular plates or extruded shapes (X, Y, Z, W Chairs); stone is sliced into thin planes or quarried in rough chunks (Cloister for Learning); glass comes in very thin plates (Apartment for Art and Music); plywood comprises standard-size flat planes (Apparel Shop). In the development of simple, direct solutions for our projects, we have incorporated the internal logic of the materials employed as a starting point for generating form. Because we exert a minimum of transformation in the journey from raw materials to finished project, the resulting forms are often basic geometric shapes that can easily be identified with the form of the raw material from which they are built.

structure

Architecture is made of matter and therefore needs a logic of structure to exist in space. Structure can contribute eloquently to architectural form, from overall building structure (Industrial Building) down to the smallest scale of detail (pivot door in the Workspace for Architects) or functional object incorporated into a project (Folded Handle). Each of the projects discussed in these pages evolves from a clear approach to structure at every level of scale and investigates the visual possibilities inherent in expressing that logic.

Our work also explores the relationship of structure to material. In the pursuit of simple, direct solutions we have come to appreciate the design potential in the symbiotic relationship between these two architectural elements. A thin plate of steel can become a rigid columnar support with a single fold (Apartment in Five Quadrants). Two notched and intersecting panels of oriented strand board can support large loads (Workplace for Publishing).

materials

Materials are the matter from which architecture is made. Both nature (wood, stone) and humankind (steel, bronze, glass) have created a wealth of options, each with its own internal logic. In our work, decisions about appropriate materials are made at the outset of each project, simultaneous with the consideration of appropriate geometry and structure. Materials are selected for their structural, visual, and tactile properties, with an eye to cost. Often innovative applications of materials evolve from budget or schedule constraints (metal-dust concrete-floor sealer in the Apparel Shop). By minimizing the complexity of the detailing, expensive materials can become affordable (stone facade and column cladding of the Cloister for Learning).

A design strategy based on these three elements is an inclusive way to make architecture, since many solutions are possible. Our design decisions are guided by the desire to minimize elaboration and let the geometry, structure, and materials speak for themselves.

geometry

In this column the ordering principles of each project are discussed. Geometry includes the spatial representation of order at many levels, from overall site configuration to plans, sections, and elevations to details and functional objects.

structure

Structure allows material to have form and order, and thus discussion of structure in each project is located in the central column. This axis of analysis also applies to all elemental scales from buildings to functional objects.

materials

Materials are the tactile reality of the built work, after it has been ordered by concepts of geometry and structure. Because materials constitute the third axis of analysis, their role in each project is examined in the third column.

Margaret Helfand Architects

Garment Showroom

ground steel plate
cherry
clear glass
sand-blasted glass
solar bronze glass
limestone
granite
recycled rubber

A showroom is a place for viewing a collection.

The function of this showroom, located in Manhattan's garment district, is to articulate the concept of clothing, provide a provocative backdrop for its presentation, and create a stimulating environment that can stand alone when the collection is out of view.

In this showroom, natural-fiber sportswear for women is seasonally presented to buyers from across the United States. The collection is located centrally, with garments displayed in rotation to seated groups of buyers. Adjacent to the showroom are spaces for ancillary functions, including a conference room and administrative offices.

Freestanding functional elements built from a variety of natural materials animate the otherwise minimally transformed space. Each element provides the opportunity to explore the:

visual
structural
tactile

properties of its signature materials:

steel
wood
glass
stone
rubber

In formulating a design solution appropriate for the program and client, several concepts emerged:

non-orthogonal geometry to suggest casualness
trapezoidal forms to recall perspectival perception of rectilinear forms
direct transformation of materials into structure
layering of materials to achieve function
use of material as color
use of material as texture
systems supported by gravity
planar structures
triangulated structures
minimized fastening

geometry

What appears to be an ad hoc plan of four primary display elements is actually a right-angle x-y-intersected double axis that has been rotated around an existing freestanding structural column.

Triangulated structural members supporting these display elements establish secondary axes that organize other elements in the space, such as the entry alcove, reception desk, and bench/coat alcove. Particular axial alignments were selected to address functional requirements or circulation clearances.

structure

Thin steel plate provides the primary vertical and horizontal support for the freestanding elements.

Lateral support for these thin planes is achieved where necessary by welding secondary planes onto the perpendicular axis.

materials

Basic building materials were selected to complement the natural fibers of the clothing.

Disk-ground steel plate, cherry, and etched, bronze, and clear glass comprise and identify the three display elements and in combination form the central storage element.

Stone, a durable surface for work and walking, was used for tabletops and flooring.

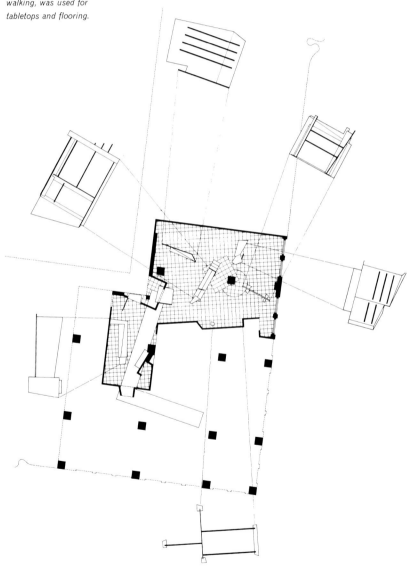

Orthogonal and non-orthogonal geometries are juxtaposed, re-inforcing the identity of each. Rather than being based on a Cartesian system of order, the functional elements of this space respect only the horizontal datum of gravity, which dictates that tabletop work surfaces, floors, and hanging bars be parallel to one another.

Tables consist of rectangular and interrelated trapezoidal shapes.

The all-steel display element is composed of three thin planes. The two vertical planes are folded in toward each other and are laterally supported at the floor by a third plane. Four bars cut from the large vertical plane and triangulated between the two vertical planes provide additional lateral support above. The bars and slots also support hangers on each side for displaying garments.

Tables were assembled from three flat planes with no mechanical fasteners. Relying exclusively on gravity and balance, a granite slab rests atop two slotted intersecting steel plates, employing an elementary form of structure similar to that used by children for card houses.

Unadorned planes of stone and steel create a dense and sensual visual reading by pre-senting to the observer their natural colors, textures, and reflective characteristics.

structure　　**materials**

*The glass display
element was assembled
from three planes of
glass balanced on
edge and propped into
vertical position by
steel pylons. No
fasteners were used.*

*The pylons consist
of two perpendicular
plates welded at right
angles and cantilevered
up from the floor.
The plate parallel to
the glass holds it in
place and is rectangular.
The secondary steel
plate provides lateral
support for the first
and is trapezoidal,
tapering toward the top
as the load diminishes.*

*The concept of layering
materials is at its most
concentrated in the
glass display fixture.
The fragility of the
three slipping layers
of bronze, etched, and
clear glass restrained
by cantilevered steel
pylons creates a mem-
orable visual statement
with minimal trans-
formation of materials.*

structure   materials

Wood panels are most
effectively used to
create hollow box
structures. In the
wood display element,
volumetric forms are
created for stability.

The natural warm
color and inherent
complexity of the wood
grain contrast with the
colors and textures of
the steel, stone, and
glass that have been
used for the other
functional elements
in the space.

geometry	structure	materials
Trapezoidal forms suggest a forced perspective view of rectilinear forms, contrasting perception with reality.		*The elegance and warmth of the steel, disk-ground by hand, is used as a backdrop for the garments and contrasts with the rough sandstone of the walking surface.*
The regularized grid of floor tiles aligned with the new diagonal wall of the showroom provides a frame of reference for the dual geometries.		*Walls and ceilings are unadorned white surfaces, reflecting the light and colors of the objects within.*
A square glass plate is pinned to the wall, overlapping the trapezoidal cutout of the entry window and hovering slightly above the stone ledge.		
	Thin planes of horizontal steel cantilever from the vertical axis to create shelving for displaying folded garments.	

Workspace for Architects

shot-blasted steel plate
wire mesh
metal dust
oriented strand board
corrugated cement board
mineral strand board
incised glass
precast terrazzo
recycled rubber

An office for architects is a place for gathering people, ideas, and resources.

Located in an 1860s townhouse in the historic Murray Hill neighborhood in midtown Manhattan, this office conducts a dialogue between the historic existing space and the new functional elements that have been inserted to accommodate new uses; the architecture for the new uses follows an independent logic. Workspace encompasses individual workstations as well as a large meeting table for collaborative work. Resources are displayed prominently in three distinct libraries:

books and periodicals on art and architecture
technical information
materials

The desire to accommodate the functional elements without disturbing the fabric of the existing architecture made the project a laboratory for experimentation:

planar structures reinforced by slotted intersections
planar structures reinforced by bending
triangulated support systems
bent-plane support systems
slotted supports in lieu of mechanical fasteners
layering of materials to achieve function
pivoting planes
segmented forms
series of progressive geometric forms

geometry

To connect the two major spaces at either end of the floor plan, a bent diagonal axis was drawn starting from the office archive at the rear and the conference room. That axis projects toward the central entry area, where it is inscribed on the floor, and reflects at an opposite but equal angle from the side wall. Continuing toward the studio space in the front, the diagonal axis is offset at the pivoting closet door and terminates in alignment with the studio flat file, the repository of current work.

The bent axis organizes and aligns the functional elements in the space: the conference table, the plan file, the inset cardboard panels at workstations, the triangular pylons supporting workstations, and the bookshelves.

The glass door to the conference room, viewed from the back in this photograph, contains a conceptual drawing, compiled in two layers, of the office. The bent axis of the overall space and triangulated alignments of the pylons supporting the workstations are carved into the first plate of glass. The second layer represents the geometries and location of the primary functional elements and delineates the shapes and layers of the segmented conference table. Flanking the scale plan to the right are unfolded elevations of the east wall, which contains the three libraries.

structure

The shelves for the book and periodical library are rectangular planks, rotated away from the wall at various angles. They are supported in space by a bent-steel-plate beam, and in order to prevent them from overturning, the necessary corners have been wedged into a continuous slot in the back wall. The steel beams bear their load on the side walls in slots fitted to their angled profile. No mechanical fasteners were used.

The shelf at the entry for incoming and outgoing packages is a bent plate suspended by gravity from a clip behind.

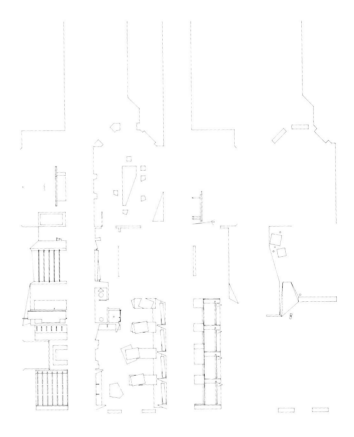

geometry **structure**

*Rectangles, some
rotated and some
segmented, order the
workstations, confer-
ence table, and shelves.*

*A rectangular confer-
ence table is bisected
diagonally by the bent
axis that organizes the
new functions within
the office. The smaller
triangular segment is
mobile and can be
used in the corner as a
console for a telephone
and small workspace,
or it can be reunited
with the larger segment
to create a larger, more
formal meeting space.*

*The eight conference-
room chairs comprise
a geometric variation
series. (See X, Y, Z, W
Chairs for further
discussion.)*

*The tabletop is can-
tilevered on all sides
from a single bent steel
plate. The cantilever is
supported by a layer of
corrugated cement
board that diagonally
spans, and extends
beyond, the table's two
legs, which are created
from the perpendicular
bend of the plate. A
layer of oriented strand
board was added above
to provide a level fin-
ish. Layers are held in
place by gravity; no
fasteners were used.*

*The triangular segment
of the table is a tripod-
frame structure assem-
bled from bent steel
plate. Cement board
was not used, as this
structure does not
employ cantilevers.*

geometry

Geometry, when perceived in a state of motion, suggests new geometries. A pivoting rectangle becomes an infinite number of trapezoids as it changes its angle in relation to the viewer.

A steel plate stiffened by folding along two edges and pinned to a vertical pole becomes a door, in a movement similar to half of a standard hinge rotating around a hinge pin.

To allow clearance for the portion of the panel that rotates within the interior, the top and bottom corners were cut away.

structure

Supported by tubular sleeves welded to bent steel plates and pinned to the back of the panel, the door rotates on three ball bearings.

The pivot pole is held in vertical position by base and head plates sleeved inside the pole and anchored to the existing wood substructure.

Inside, a square steel rod for hanging rests, held by gravity, within a bent-steel-plate shelf structure.

materials

Steel plate and bar stock were utilized with their basic mill-scale finish. Special components for attachment were ground to expose the raw material. Linear strip-bolts fabricated to transfer the weight of the door to the ball bearings are bronze, a more noble metal, used to resist corrosion.

previous pages:
Removable panels of standard-size cardboard for cutting surfaces are anchored within the work surfaces by a rotated rectangular recess, which engages two corners.

The function of trash storage was subjected to the same rigorous process of analysis and problem solving as other elements. Thin plastic liners are suspended in space by coiled and bolted lengths of coarse woven wire mesh. The rectangular mesh panels were overlapped with slightly different offsets to create varied but conceptually related conical forms.

previous pages:
Exploring structural concepts initiated in the Garment Showroom (1987), the functional elements are constructed of simple planes. Materials are layered and leaned against each other and held in place by gravity rather than with mechanical fasteners.

The library shelving and table in the studio were constructed from notched intersecting panels of oriented strand board, using traditional egg-crate technology. At the materials library, shelving slides through slots and cantilevers out beyond the support pylon to create a place for displaying new samples.

previous pages:
Common building materials, selected for their economy and structural properties, were combined as necessary to construct the functional elements. Oriented strand board was used for vertical structural members supporting workstations and shelving and for horizontal work surfaces. Steel was used where greater strength was required or where a simple bent plate provided a more economical solution. Corrugated cement panels were used for long spans, for cantilevers, or where great rigidity was required.

Workstations and overhead shelving are suspended from freestanding triangular pylons of oriented strand board. A layer of corrugated cement, slotted into the pylons, supports desktops and shelving.

Each of the three support points consists of a steel plate bent and welded to a section of steel tubing, following the principle of a knuckle hinge riding on a continuous hinge pin. The tubing sits on a large ball-bearing ring supported by a small section of tubing fastened with set screws to the pole. The steel tubing rides on a self-lubricating tubular bronze bushing, exposed to view at the top.

The vertical edges of the door panel were bent at right angles to provide stiffness for the thin plate.

A steel plate was bent to form a shelf and rod support.

Several steel finishes were employed. The door and shelf panels retain the dark mill scale from the rolling process. The pole and tubular sleeves reveal a finer texture from the machining process. The bent-plate bracket was disk-ground, expressing the high level of the artisan's effort required to create these hardware elements.

Two bronze alloys were used. The acorn-head nuts on the inside, threaded rod between, and strip plate exposed on the outside of the door panel were fabricated from a commercial bronze alloy that has a golden color. The higher copper content of the bronze tubing of the bushing eases the rotation of the door and creates a more reddish color in the alloy.

X, Y, Z, W Chairs

ground steel
shot-blasted steel

A chair is a structure for suspending the body in space.

In its simplest terms, a chair consists of a seat, a back, and legs. In this series, various geometric forms were explored.

Comfort in a chair can be achieved with two flat planes if the seat is inclined properly in relation to the floor and the back is angled properly in relation to the seat. A chair can thus be created from a single plate, bent at the division between seat and back, and placed in a skeletal frame. Stable support for the seat and back element can be furnished by a four-leg frame, elevating it a comfortable distance above the floor.

In this geometric variation series, rectangular steel plates equal in size were cut and bent along the orthogonal or diagonal to create four pairs of chairs, each with a unique but related form; the frames are identical. The cutting and bending follow a progression starting with the X Chair. The steel plate for the X Chair was cut on a diagonal. The two trapezoidal halves were bent to create two mirror-image chairs, with seats wider than backs. The remaining operations, for the Y, Z, and W Chairs, explore the geometric shapes that derive from cutting and bending according to various parallel and diagonal alignments.

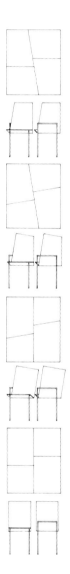

Apartment in Five Quadrants

ground steel plate
radiator screens
purpleheart
cherry
dichroic glass
iridescent handblown glass
ribbed glass
glass-and-copper-dust tile
granite

A home is a place to accommodate the body and refresh the spirit.

Located within the boundaries of an existing apartment in a landmark 1920s building on Riverside Drive in New York City, this home is a setting for work, play, and the usual domestic functions. At the same time, it provides a contemplative environment.

The minimal amount of space in this apartment challenged traditional assumptions about static functional solutions. Functions were concentrated into three independent but geometrically related freestanding elements:

> sleeping/dressing
> sitting/working
> dining

These divisions allow for separation of activities while encouraging the development of a language of interrelated forms, structure, and materials to integrate the space.

Each element is self-supporting and composed of wood and steel, with each material selected to perform its most efficient structural function. Planes of overlapping translucent glass perform two functions: they provide optional screening for openings to service areas, and they visually and physically connect the new architecture to the existing space.

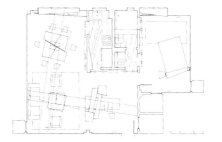

The concept of motion was introduced to provide variability. The occupant could: open, close, or change the overlap of the glass; alter the position of lights suspended from a tension wire system above; rotate the television to address the dining table, sitting area, or desk; adjust the angle of the desk resting on the bookcase; rotate the angle of the bed in relation to the wall; or open or close the segmented table.

The functional elements evolve from basic structural concepts investigated in prior work:

> bending
> layering
> sliding
> pivoting
> cantilevering
> pinning
> resting

Several new ideas about perception and materiality were also explored:

> translucence
> reflectance
> natural color contrast
> layering glass textures
> motion

geometry

The logic of the plan is simple. New functions are accommodated within freestanding elements. The elements are aligned in relation to a new Cartesian system that has been overlaid onto and rotated from the existing structure in order to provide more comfortable circulation in the space. Where new forms refer back to the existing order, trapezoids are created.

The activities in each quadrant are accommodated with an independent functional element. The footprint of each element is encoded in each adjacent pair of sliding glass panels.

structure

The process used to fuse the layers of glass also meets safety-glass standards for laminated glass.

materials

The three types of glass layered in each panel were produced by different processes. Dichroic glass is made from two sheets of plate glass laminated with a dichroic metallic additive in the liquid vinyl interlayer. Ribbed glass is pressed into molds to create texture. The hand-blowing of the iridescent glass results in uneven texture and air bubbles.

The shifting overlap of shapes in each panel and between moving panels allows for an infinite number of visual variations.

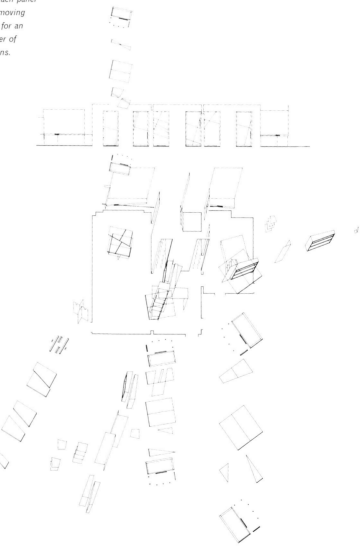

The four quadrants of the tabletop rest on ledges attached to the pair of bent-steel bases. The steel edge of the bases is exposed flush with the top of the table. To further illustrate the structural system this narrow separation of wood quadrants remains as a void space where the top cantilevers beyond the bases.

The thin dimension of the steel bases contrasts with the thickness of the solid cherry top. Separation of the top into four independent quadrants allows for thermal movement of the wood.

The dining table transforms a simple square into a rectangle while respecting the rotated geometry of the new functional elements of the space. The square rotates along the axis of the new elements. The top is subdivided into four trapezoidal quadrants following the pair of offset bent steel plates that forms the base. To enlarge the table, the two halves open along the axis of rotation and a parallelogram leaf is inserted. With this final operation the table is resolved into a simple rectangular shape.

The large expanse of unadorned wood contrasts with the gleam of the ground-steel pylons and soft glow of the shifting glass planes.

To create the load-bearing, spanning, and cantilevering components required to construct the free-standing functional elements, minimal structural systems were investigated.

Bent-steel-plate pylons provide vertical support for all elements: the bedroom|dressing| library unit, the library|video|desk unit, the dining table, and the coffee table. Horizontal steel plates welded to pylons provide lateral support for the pylons and serve as shelves.

Wood-plank shelving units span the space between the pylons, acting as box beams. Shelf units are pinned to the pylons at the back or sides with a triangulated pattern of three small bronze acorn-head bolts.

Steel shelves are cantilevered and fastened to the pylons with welded moment connections.

Materials were selected for their inherent structural properties. Steel, highly efficient structurally, was used for load-bearing elements. Wood, easily fabricated into volumetric forms, was used for long-span shelving.

Color, texture, and surface reflectance provide visual stimulation and emphasize the inherent properties of the materials employed.

geometry

A central service quadrant incorporating kitchen and bath becomes a lantern, wrapped in shifting planes of light transmitted and reflected through translucent glass. Almost a perfect cube, the lantern orders the surrounding space into four adjacent quadrants of similar size, each with a specific function: sleeping, working, sitting, and eating.

The Cartesian axes organizing the new functional elements cross in the sitting area, marked by the bent-steel angled base of the coffee table. The two rotated layers of glass that form the tabletop reiterate the relationship of the two geometries of the apartment. One layer follows the orthogonal geometry of the existing building; the other follows the rotated geometry of the new construction.

Above, crossing through the space, the two low-voltage wire lighting systems also mark the intersection of the rotated axes.

structure

Shifting planes of glass are pinned to bent-steel frames with purpleheart cubes and cherry strips. Frames roll on ball bearings and are guided above in wood tracks cantilevered from the wall on bent-steel brackets,

The steel table base demonstrates how a single fold can transform a simple plane into a structural element.

The radiator and air-conditioner unit below the window are screened by a layer of wire coil drape suspended from a rod attached to a cantilevered window sill made from bent steel plate.

materials

Layers of dichroic, handblown, and pressed glass were laminated to create safety glass for rolling screens. Layers of each panel were collaged in patterns to describe a segment of the adjacent floor plan.

Light, used here as a material, transforms the panels. They glow softly when backlit or emit intense flashes of color when light is reflected directly off the surface.

Two woods of contrasting color define the functional elements. Purpleheart was used for the more formal sitting area and other special details; cherry was used elsewhere.

Glass, an extremely rigid material, is capable of long cantilevers when counterbalanced across a fulcrum.

The library|video|desk element employs several minimal structural systems that relate directly to the materials used. Bent steel plate is used for the two major pylons, the cantilevered shelves for audio-video components, and the desk. Books, videotapes, and speakers are contained in wood-plank box-beam shelf units that span the space between the pylons.

To emphasize the functional differences of the two sides of the structure, contrasting species of wood were used. Purpleheart, the rarer species, was used for the sitting-area side while cherry was used for the desk side.

Two rectangular steel plates are bent and upended to provide support for a desk, shelving, and rotating video monitor. Other components, in steel and wood, are rectangles or trapezoids that appropriately accommodate their functions.

geometry

*The Cartesian grid
of tiles recalls the
axial organization of
the project. Within the
service core, however,
axes align with the
building structure.
The diagonal jamb at
the interior window
connects the bathing
space to the sleeping
space; that opening
allows the television
to be viewed from
the tub.*

materials

*Reflective glass-and-
copper-dust tiles cover
surfaces where the
light is refracted
through water.*

*Granite slabs provide
an impermeable and
durable surface for
ledges.*

*Optional privacy
between the bathing
and sleeping areas
is achieved with a
movable translucent
glass panel.*

*The pylon-and-shelf
unit pivots away from
the wall in deference to
the rotated axes of the
new architecture and
to allow circulation
space for the bed and
dressing area behind.
Orientation of the bed
allows direct views to
the window and the
corner television.*

Industrial Building

structural steel
formed sheet steel
aluminum
foil-faced insulation
vinyl-faced insulation
glass
corrugated fiberglass
concrete
crushed stone

An industrial building is a simple, flexible container.

The straightforward program for flexible industrial space provided the opportunity to explore several fundamental architectural operations:

> containing
> spanning
> extruding
> bisecting, reversing, slipping
> minimizing

The most elementary structural system to enclose a large space is the single-span steel frame. Wrapped with a light-gauge corrugated-steel skin, this becomes the prototypical industrial shed.

Geometric manipulations such as bisecting, reversing, and slipping the halves of this form result in architecture that relates harmoniously to its rural setting, with surrounding valleys and hills, and to other utilitarian structures.

Elegance resides in the simplicity of the basic elements:

> structural subdivisions of concrete slab
> tapered steel framing
> repetitive rhythm of purlins
> cable cross-bracing
> fold-up service door

Clustering the service elements back-to-back in a cube along one side provides the maximum amount of clear floor area and, if required, allows the structure to be subdivided into two parts. Double-height volumes along the high ends allow for the future development of office space at a mezzanine level.

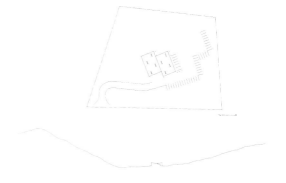

geometry

Simple sheds and primary volumes are a familiar vocabulary for large structures in rural environments.

structure

A roof plane was suspended over the personnel entrance to create a canopy. An assemblage of building-system fragments, the plane hangs from threaded rods resting in wall framing beyond and was triangulated for stability with threaded-rod tie-downs.

materials

Standard tubular aluminum storefront components were utilized in a geometric rhythm to create a large glazed opening at the primary entrance.

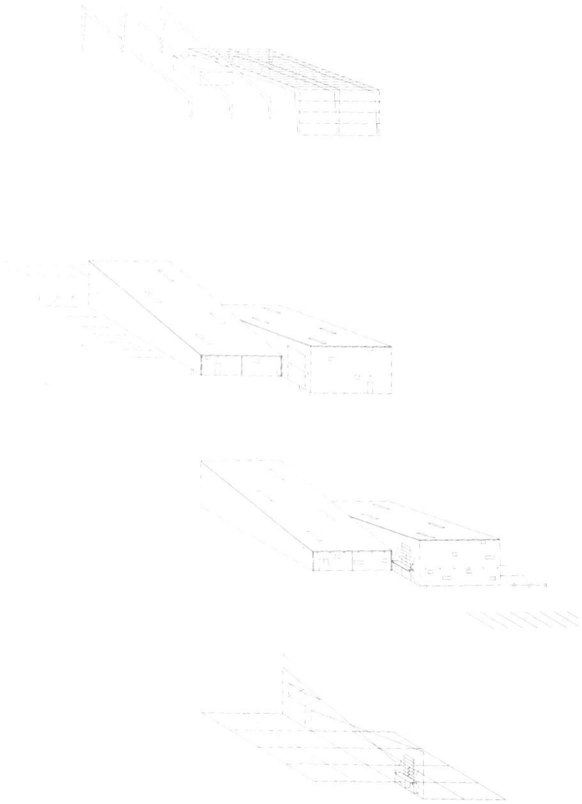

geometry   materials

The folding motion
of the overhead door
recalls the motions of
cutting, reversing, and
slipping that were used
to generate the original
form of the building.

Although the texture of
the roofing and siding
remains consistent
throughout the build-
ing, the color shifts
from white to galva-
nized on the walls
along the central axis
of the slipping wedges
and on the sloping
surfaces of the roof.

The flat plane of the
door, when folded up,
creates a projecting
canopy over the load-
ing activities below.

Crushed local stone
creates a finely tex-
tured foreground for
the sleekness of the
metal membrane.

Galvanized-pipe
bollards give scale to
the elevations and pro-
tect the building's skin
from vehicular impact.

The repetitive logic
of framing members
is fully exposed on
the interior of the
container.

Economy of means
dictated the geometry
of the steel framing,
which was engineered
and fabricated by the
building systems man-
ufacturer. No steel
was used that is not
structurally essential.

Overlapping of the
slipped-wedge struc-
tures is visible from
the interior along the
center axis and creates
unexpected residual
forms.

The square grid of
concrete cold-joints
inscribes the basic
geometry of the build-
ing in the floor. A
checkerboard system
of concrete placement
allowed the first set
of slabs to be used as
formwork for the
second set.

Interior finishes reflect
their structural or func-
tional requirements.
Rust-inhibiting paint
gives color to steel
structural members.
Float-finish concrete
also serves as a high-
load-bearing floor
structure. Following
the color algorithm of
the exterior, wall and
roof insulation provide
two additional finishes:
fiberglass batts with foil
facing are used at the
roof and center-axis
walls where galvanizing
is used on the exterior,
and white vinyl facing
is used on other
vertical surfaces where
the metal siding on the
outside is white.

The central service core
was constructed from
light-gauge steel and
drywall and was painted
white, with black-and-
white checkerboard tile
on the floor.

geometry

In plan, the two slipped wedges forming the envelope of the building are two halves of a square. The square is subdivided into a four-square structural grid, which is visible from the interior.

The slipping of the two halves by one structural bay creates a personnel entrance along the central axis on one side and a freight entrance on the opposite side.

The slope of the roof results in single-story space on one side of each wedge and double-height space on the opposite side.

Corrugated skylight panels were inserted into the roof planes in a checkerboard pattern, centered on the grid modules.

structure

From the exterior, the clear-span roof structure is evident, but the pattern of framing elements is concealed behind the flush membrane of the envelope.

materials

Light-gauge standing-seam metal roofing and siding seamlessly enclose all surfaces, emphasizing the nature of the building as container.

Corrugations create a rhythm of shadow as the sun moves across the building, bringing the dimension of time to an otherwise static structure.

Art Museum

1991

brick
copper
aluminum
glass
granite
bluestone

A museum is an environment that engages viewer and object.

A renowned college art museum, located in a historic district of Providence, Rhode Island, required new gallery space to accommodate large sculpture and small objects including textiles and works on paper. The available site was an L-shaped space next to the existing museum, an accretion of several adjacent structures stepping down a steep hill.

In grafting contemporary architecture onto the traditional fabric of the existing museum, fundamental features of the original architecture were respected:

> primary geometric forms in massing
> sloping roof shapes
> brick walls
> copper roofs
> stone site walls

The simple solution evolved through experimentation with several concepts explored in earlier projects:

> bipartite massing
> rotation
> slipping
> folding
> wrapping

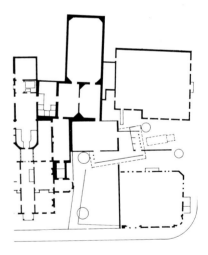

The program resolved into two major elements. The gallery for sculpture and installation art required a large flexible volume with high ceilings and north light. This became the primary, rectangular mass nesting against two perpendicular walls of existing galleries. Overhead, the clear-span truss system was rotated to allow for north-facing vertical glazing in the sawtooth roof.

Textiles and works on paper require more intimate spaces with minimal, controlled lighting and lower ceilings. The functions were accommodated in the secondary volume, which wraps around the primary gallery. This form is also a rectangle, though it is carved away where it overlaps the primary rectangle and is rotated to provide clearance for a much-used path between the new building and an existing college building on the corner. The roof is also a folded-plate form, but it consists of a smaller-scale sawtooth and, rather than being glazed along each truss to achieve an even field of light below, is glazed only at the exposed ends where it folds up to create small triangular voids.

The offset of the two rectangular masses signals the two functional points of entry. A public entrance faces the primary street and is approached through the outdoor sculpture court. Around the corner, a service entrance and loading dock serving the entire museum are recessed from the street.

In order to link visually these new forms to the existing museum and other historic structures of the neighborhood, brick, copper, and stone were used to wrap walls, roofs, and site walls.

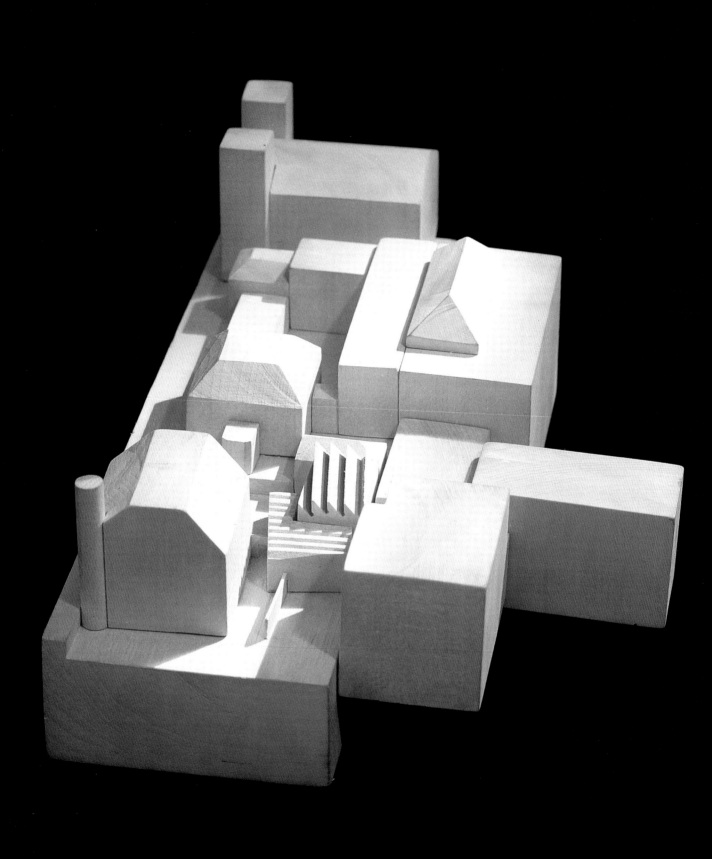

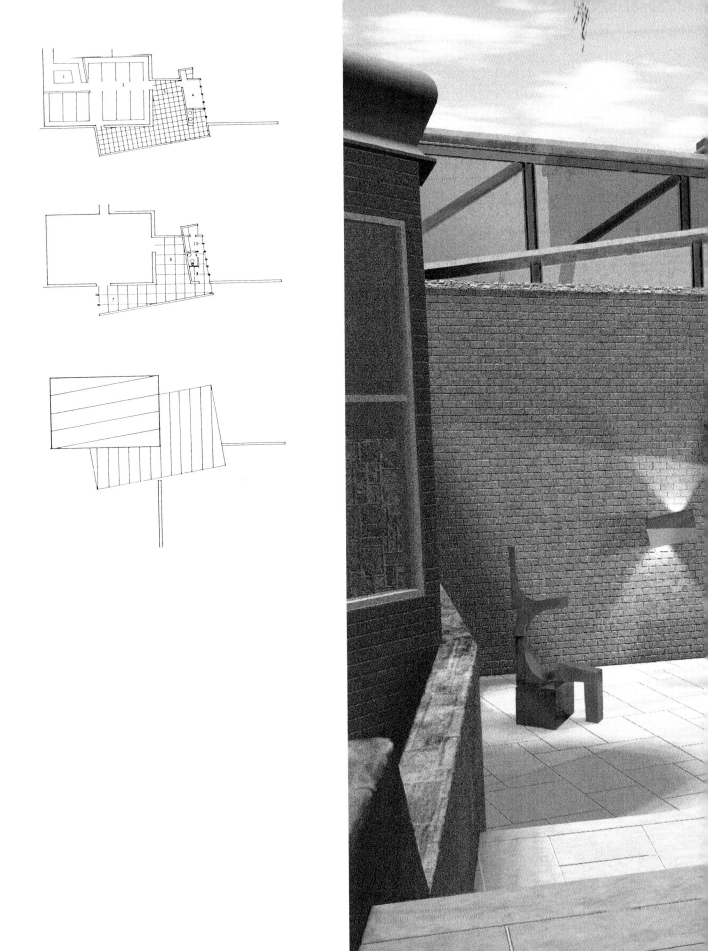

Apparel Shop

steel plate
bronze plate
braided-bronze-wire rope
bronze dust
steel dust
cherry
oriented strand board
bent glass
concrete

A shop engenders the desire to acquire.

Suspending garments in space is the abstracted yet essential function accommodated in this project, a shop for avant-garde European and Japanese designer apparel for men and women in Santa Monica, California.

Pursuit of an obvious solution of the utmost simplicity and requisite elegance led to experiments in:

suspending
anchoring
spanning
supporting

A tension-cable system for hanging crisscrosses the perimeter of the space, with intermediate support provided by movable pylons. These folded steel plates also provide visual punctuation, creating groupings of suspended garments.

Intrusions of existing structural and mechanical elements along walls and ceilings necessitated an exploration of:

folding
wrapping

The resulting concealment simultaneously performs other active program functions, creating spaces for storage and display, and mirrored surfaces.

The ad hoc locations of these intrusions create an internal logic of zones within the space, which is reinforced by the loosely checkered floor pattern and undulating ceiling.

geometry	structure	materials

The geometry of the shop is based on rotated and folded rectangles. In plan, trapezoids are formed when these rectangles, denoted by the two-color floor checkerboard, intersect with the existing orthogonal walls of the space.

A linear display system is created with overlapping lines crisscrossing along the perimeter. This system of overlapping lines is reinforced by the low-voltage lighting wires overhead.

Folded planes of gypsum board at the ceiling conceal suspended mechanical equipment and piping while creating zones within the space.

Planes of cherry project into the space, concealing structural elements and storage areas as well as providing the background with visual variation.

Cherry islands float through the space, displaying folded goods.

Bronze dust and steel dust suspended within clear concrete sealer were used as floor finishes over the exposed structural slab to provide a minimal but appropriate complement to the bronze-and-steel infrastructure of the space. The two colors were used to indicate the rotated checkerboard organization of the space.

previous page:
Cherry, laminated into large panels, was used for the dressing-room doors.

The interior of the dressing rooms was treated like a garment lining. Oriented strand board, a less dressy material than cherry, was used. It was finished, however, with a bronze-dust stain.

Bent bronze plate was fabricated to create door pulls and mounting hardware for the pivoting panels.

previous page:
The checkerboard organization of the space carries through the dressing area.

The corners of the dressing rooms are efficiently used for triangular seats and hanging rods, which span the space between two adjacent walls.

previous page:

Pivoting planes suspended from pipe columns form closures for dressing rooms.

Rods, constructed of copper pipe and held by gravity, sit in circular cutouts.

geometry

Floating display elements are rectangles, but their rectangular glass tops are rotated above, creating trapezoidal overhangs.

Rectangles of wood paneling along the perimeter were used to conceal existing structural and mechanical elements. When the rectangles terminate at a sloping ceiling, trapezoids are formed.

Pylons, created by folding a rectangular steel plate on a diagonal, appear as two trapezoids in elevation.

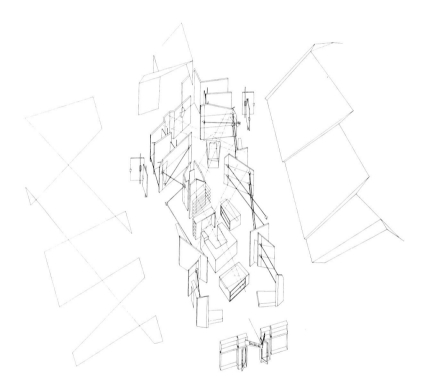

geometry	structure	materials

Bronze-wire rope, crisscrossing two sides of the space, is the material in closest proximity to the merchandise. Two rows for half-height hanging are used on the men's side while a single, lower row is used to hang full-length women's garments.

The principal structural system of the space is the network of tension cables, which support significant weight over long spans. The ends of the cables are anchored into slots in the steel brackets; the wedge-shaped steel washers allow the incoming angle of the cable to be adjusted. Length and tension can be manipulated with a threaded fitting at the termination cap.

Steel plate with an integral mill-scale finish was bent diagonally to form movable pylons. The pylons provide intermediate support for the tension cables and create divisions between groups of merchandise.

Cherry paneling made from standard-size plywood creates orthogonal gridded planes at different orientations throughout the space, giving scale and rhythm to the experience of moving through the shop.

Planes of glass rest atop the steel brackets that anchor the cables, spanning the corners to create display alcoves.

Speakers were concealed simply by slicing away a corner of the paneling and inserting a triangular frame covered with speaker cloth.

Native characteristics of the materials are visible at close range: wood grain resulting from growth patterns and veneer slicing, mill scale from the steel-rolling process, twisting in braided bronze rope. Contrasts of color, texture, and reflectivity are intended to stimulate perception of fabrics, textures, and garment shapes.

The weight of the garments is transmitted through gravity systems—from suspended hanger to tension cable to slotted pylon to floor —using no mechanical fasteners.

The angularity of the elements in the setting contrasts with the curvilinear forms of the natural human body.

Folded Corner Sconce

bronze plate
sand-blasted glass

A sconce is a discreet source of light.

The need for high-intensity indirect lighting that provides efficient distribution but is not obtrusively located on walls or ceilings led to the development of this new approach. By locating a high-wattage quartz halogen light source in the corner of a room, light could be reflected back into the space from the walls and ceiling.

A simple folded bronze plate was used to shield the bulb and socket from view, provide mounting for the socket, attach the fixture to the wall, and receive the glass diffuser.

A plate of acid-etched glass was folded once to create a two-sided shape that allows the light to be diffused along the two axes defined by the corner.

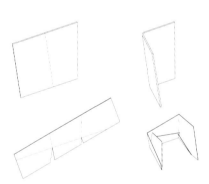

Folded Corner Sconce • 86

10 Vessels

1992

bronze plate
steel ballast

A vessel is an object for containing.

In the ongoing exploration of simple solutions for architectural problems, the folded plane is often an efficient approach. Structural stability can be achieved with a minimum quantity of material and a minimal amount of transformation.

We experimented with a series of forms exploring the formal and functional possibilities inherent in cutting and folding a thin bronze plate according to specific geometric relationships. We found that a container can be created simply by folding the edges of a flat plane upward to enclose space; the quantity and shape of the space vary depending on the horizontal dimension of the base, the vertical dimension of the sides, and the relationship between the two.

A square of sheet metal was inscribed with a slightly smaller square and rotated at an angle that expresses the difference in dimension of the outer and inner squares. The material that fell outside the intersection of the corners was removed and the remainder bent upward at twice the angle of rotation of the inner square.

Each successive vessel was constructed from a slightly larger square of metal, while the inner square became smaller by an equal increment. As the base becomes smaller, the sides fold upward at an increasing angle. In addition, the corners of the base were moved incrementally out of alignment with the inner square, thus creating an increasingly irregular trapezoidal base, which by the seventh base became a triangle.

The uses for each vessel evolve from the first, a tray form, through bowl forms to the last two, vertical baskets that require a loose steel ballast to maintain stability.

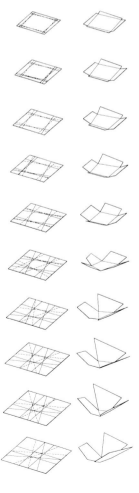

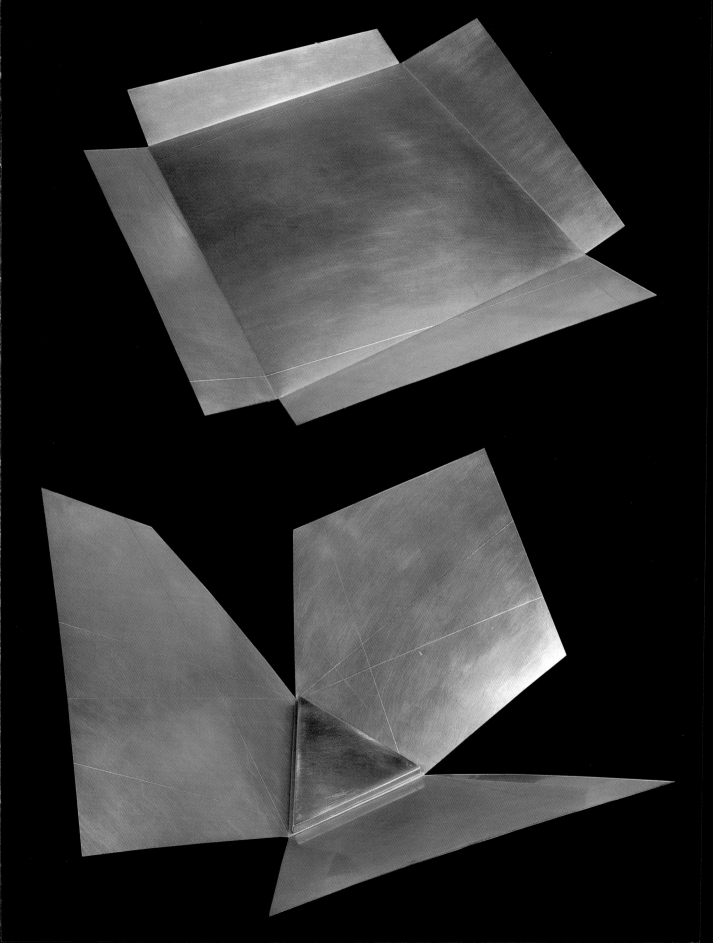

Preassembled School

buff brick
iron-spot brick
precast concrete
aluminum
maple
mineral strand board
dichroic glass
fiberglass panels
ground rubber

A teaching school is a place for children and adults to learn from each other.

The repetitive module of the classroom made this early-childhood education center at a New York City community college a good candidate for preassembled construction. Perched on a steeply sloping site at the edge of the campus next to a wooded area, the two-story structure could be entered at grade at the upper level while the classrooms at the lower level could also open onto an outdoor activity area.

The architecture of the project came to embody the essential duality of the educational process: the simultaneous needs for order, logic, and predictability and for creativity, intuition, and surprise.

Representing order and logic, the preassembled construction technology suggested certain design principles:

> stacking
> wrapping
> rectangular massing
> flat roof forms
> panelized components
> articulated field joints
> modular materials

The three blocks of classrooms at the lower level organize the building and create a square void at the center. This space, with its translucent, panelized, field-installed roof, becomes an indoor activity area for the children and a meeting space for the school.

Each classroom consists of two factory-assembled units that fall within the dimensions allowable for transport. On site, the units are interconnected and stacked. All interior and exterior finishes are installed in the factory except along the joints between the units.

The brick veneer on the exterior of the building is enlivened by using two slightly different shades of brick. Within each color zone there are also sections of contrasting joint patterns, further emphasizing the concept of wrapping. The brick installed in the field at the construction joints is given its own identity by shifting the pattern as well as by shifting the plane to projecting (at vertical joints) or recessed (at horizontal joints and parapets).

Representing creativity and surprise, contrasting design principles were employed:

> non-orthogonal geometry
> non-repetitive elements
> irregular spaces

The entry and the circulation pattern introduce the element of surprise, contrasting with the regularity of the massing and the window openings of the factory-built components. The rotated-cube entry vestibule, the rotated stair and mezzanine cutout, and the shaped atrium roof are field-installed elements that can easily follow a different geometric logic.

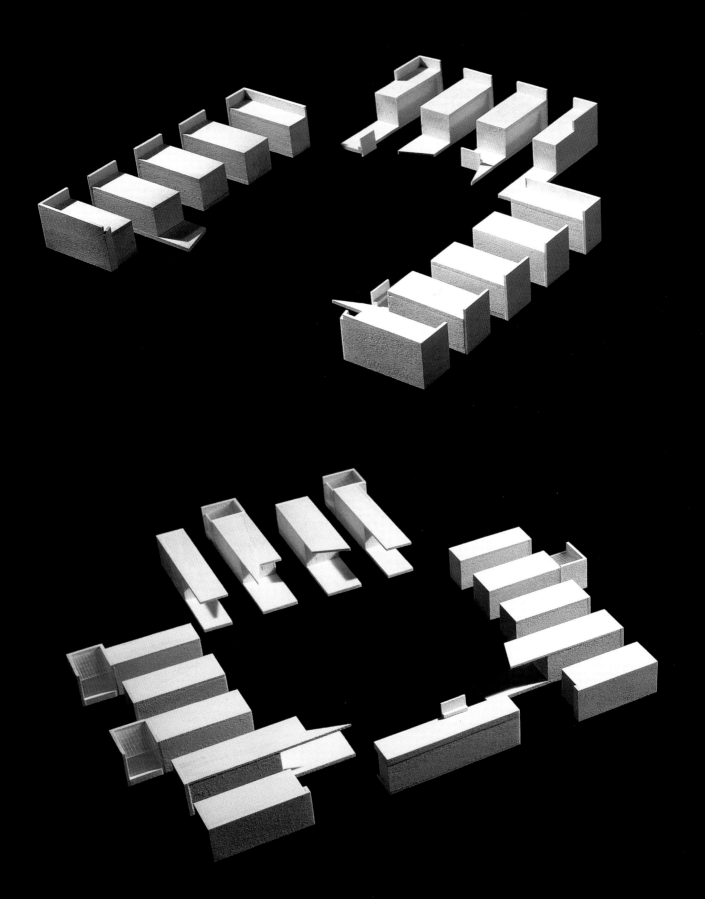

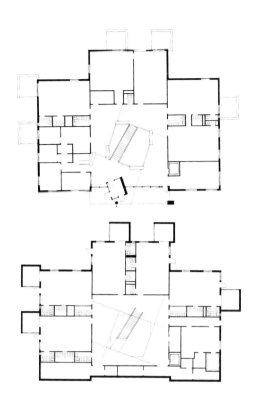

Vertical House on a Trapezoidal Site

1993

shot-blasted steel plate
bronze plate
braided bronze cable
zebrawood
maple
quartzite
slate

A house is a place to accommodate daily life with grace.

Situated at an intersection of two roads in the bottom of a canyon in Southern California, the existing house received an interior reconfiguration to complement the occupants' lifestyle.

The project encompassed several existing features:

> trapezoidal site
> four-level structure
> large glazed openings

Drawing on these givens, the project took shape as a series of interrelated functional elements within the existing loftlike spaces.

The stair is the major element linking the three living levels. The living levels, largely open in plan, were conceived as shelves floating within a simple trapezoidal cabinet. A language of lightness appropriate to the climate and the occupants' lifestyle developed, using concepts explored in earlier work:

> bent-plate structures
> tension-wire structures
> dual geometries
> freestanding functional elements

Continuity was achieved through a consistent palette of materials and a coherent language of folded planes and crisscrossing lines moving up through the vertical space.

Functional zones within the free plan are marked by freestanding cabinetry and furniture, the geometry of which reflects the axes of the trapezoidal site.

geometry

Immediately upon entering, the stair indicates the dual geometry of the house. Built on a trapezoidal corner site with no setback from the property lines, the house rises four levels from a common footprint.

The floors are conceived as shelves in a cabinet. Spaces are given little enclosure but are demarcated by functional elements, which rise only as high as necessary, thus allowing interior views above and around and creating a continuum of space spiraling up the stairway. Like a cat's cradle, a pair of low-voltage lighting wires crisscrosses the stairwell.

Interpenetration of space is evident throughout the house. The thinness of the floor edges is emphasized, turning the floors into floating planes.

The freestanding kitchen, wrapped in wood paneling, screens itself from the dining area. Embedded along the dining side is a cabinet with drawers and a surface for serving.

The segmented table reflects the trapezoidal geometry of the site. However, recombination of the segments in different orientations results in more familiar shapes, including a rectangle and a parallelogram, or three smaller groups of those forms. In this house, the smaller segments are used elsewhere until required to accommodate a larger group.

structure

The edge of the stairwell is disengaged from the tubular steel column to emphasize the horizontality of the floor plates.

A single bent steel plate supports each segment of the table independently.

materials

Because of its ability to carry heavy loads with a minimum of cross-sectional support, steel was utilized for the stair. A bent-plate asymmetrical stringer carries a folded plate, forming a continuous ribbon of risers and treads. Solid maple planks are set on top as finish treads.

The kitchen becomes a folding screen of zebrawood, concealing views from the entry and dining area beyond. A coat closet with a pivoting door is embedded in the screen construction.

The use of a single material in the independent elements creates an emphasis on form as well as on the properties of materials. Metals are appropriate for structural elements such as stairs or table bases. Wood is appropriate for constructing more complex elements, such as cabinets, or elements where a warmer surface is welcome, such as tabletops.

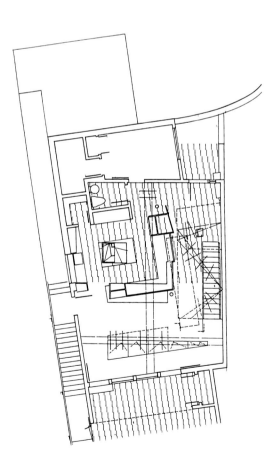

geometry	structure	materials

The dual geometry of the house organizes the elements of the kitchen. A square island is enclosed by the folding-screen wall, which contains storage and work space.

The grid of flooring refers to the axial alignment of the entry wall while the square island refers to the primary axis of the street.

Except for the hood, the kitchen elements are freestanding. High and deep closets anchor each end and provide lateral support for the screen wall of cabinets.

The hood is a folded-sheet-metal form, suspended from the ceiling and supported laterally by a series of tension cables triangulating between hood and ceiling.

Zebrawood, selected for its vibrant pattern of light and dark lines, emphasizes the folding-screen character of the perimeter kitchen element.

Atop the island, a thick slab of quartzite, with its rough finish and crystalline depth, represents the age-old significance of the kitchen hearth.

geometry	structure	materials

The light tones of the maple flooring and stair treads contrast with the dark, garnet-blasted finish of the steel. Bronze shelves and braided wire rope provide a reflective contrast.

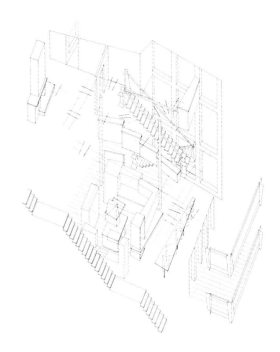

The vertical spine of circulation is the organizing axis of the project. The three living levels of the house are connected with a folded-plate single-run stair at each level.

The first run addresses the wall on the entry side without being attached to it. The second run parallels the primary geometry of the house, which aligns with the major street around the corner.

Rectangular steel plates, folded to become trapezoids, form balusters at the stair landings.

Stairs supported by bent-plate stringers connect the different levels. The stringers are anchored with surface-mounted bent plates at the edges of the stairwell.

Tension-wire railings at stairs and balconies are anchored to pylons with bent shapes that provide lateral resistance for the horizontal loads. Bronze plates welded to the legs of the pylons near the top reinforce the pylons and create a shelf at each landing.

Segmented Table

shot-blasted steel plate
bronze dust
multi-ply maple veneer

A table is a basic functional element of daily life.

Tables are the locus of concentrated activity in both the home and the workplace. Flexibility for multiple uses can become an important component.

A segmented table can accommodate varying numbers of people. It can also provide the flexibility of multiple configurations when segmented geometrically in recombinant forms: a rectangle divided longitudinally on the diagonal and laterally in equal segments can also become a parallelogram by reversing the longitudinal alignment. Both the rectangle and the parallelogram, when separated by each lateral division, can become equally dimensioned smaller units of geometry similar to the single larger unit; the two halves, when divided longitudinally, can be positioned in line to create a long narrow trapezoid; addition or subtraction of segments can create a larger or smaller form in any variant configuration.

Use of this geometry for a table creates great flexibility and adaptability. The parts can be assembled as required for large, medium, or small groups, whether for meeting or dining, while any parts not required can be used elsewhere, individually or combined for other functions.

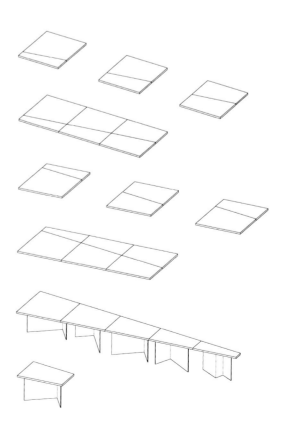

Folded Handle

1993

bronze plate

A door handle is an object that allows interaction between architecture and user.

With current accessibility regulations, lever handles for doors—rather than knobs—have become the universal standard. Lever handles have traditionally been designed as decorative hardware. A simpler solution, however, seems desirable.

By simply folding a rectangular plate on a slight diagonal, a form comfortable to the hand can be made. This form is equally effective for turning a latch or as a single pull on a door with a magnetic or ball catch.

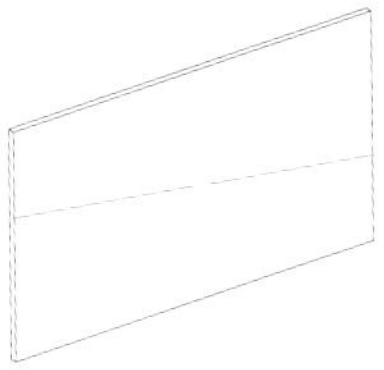

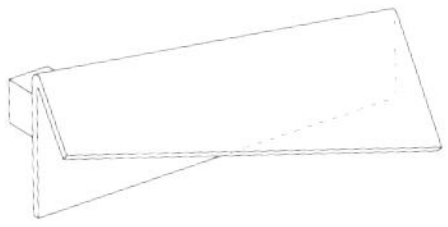

Apartment for Art and Music

shot-blasted steel plate
bronze plate
cherry
purpleheart
sand-blasted glass
ribbed glass
seeded glass
glass-and-copper-dust tile
granite

An environment for a lover of art and music provides stimulation for eye and mind.

The existing space of the trapezoidal corner apartment on the Upper East Side of Manhattan was stripped down to its bare essentials of parquet floor and plaster ceiling moldings, and reconfigured with a series of shifting planes of glass. These planes, positioned in different locations along their intersecting perpendicular axes, create partial screening or complete separation of spaces.

The perimeters of the spaces become wood-paneled wrappers, containing storage or zones for art and books.

Several concepts introduced in earlier projects are given further investigation:

layering
slipping
overlapping
wrapping
segmenting

Rather than isolating functional elements as freestanding objects, in this project the opposite approach was taken. Here, the functional elements become the boundaries of the space and were developed as a flush rhythmic surface of wood doors, panels, and partially exposed recessed shelves. The modulation of the surface is an interplay between the dual geometries defined by the trapezoidal floor plan.

Apartment for Art and Music • 106

geometry

The seven-degree alignment at the glass edges, wood doors, and ceiling mounting bars for the light fixture delineates the secondary orientation established by the trapezoidal geometry of the building.

The overlapping shapes of glass and frames create an abstract composition reflecting the geometries of the space. Repositioning the glass panels along the wood wall and against each other creates an infinity of possible variations.

materials

Comparative properties of different glass types are evident on close inspection. Each method of manufacture creates different surface and interior characteristics, which in turn reflect and transmit light to different effect.

geometry	structure	materials

Overhead guides for the glass screens are cantilevered from existing engaged beams on bent-steel brackets or from the underside of free-spanning beams.

Glass is pinned to bent-steel frames with small wood blocks.

Layers of clear, etched, ribbed, and handblown reeded glass reflect the geometry of the floor plan.

Curly-cherry paneling creates a pale russet glow behind the glass planes positioned in front.

Intersecting perpendicular axes marking the pathways of slipping translucent planes organize the space into functional zones.

Carpets, constructed of vegetable-dyed, handspun yarn and metal fibers, inscribe the geometry of the plan onto the floor plane.

The major elements of the space follow the primary orthogonal system of the building structure. A secondary geometry, however, is defined by the edge of the building overlooking the East River, which runs at a seven-degree angle to Manhattan's street grid. The expression of this geometry was reserved for vertical surfaces, allowing the plan to follow a simple Cartesian order.

The intersection of the organizing axes is marked in the floor and ceiling by the pathways on which the glass screens travel. Along the primary axis, the planes of translucent glass overlay the wood storage wrapper in an infinite number of variations of overlapping geometries.

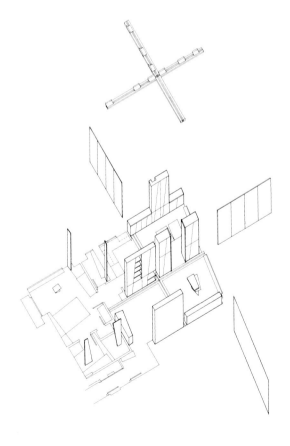

geometry	structure	materials
The rectangular top of the dining table aligns with the primary geometry of the space. It is bisected at an angle parallel to the wall beyond, which follows the East River.		
When closed, the table exposes a seven-degree void. With the installation of the trapezoidal leaf, however, the table once again becomes a continuous rectangle. When not in use, the cherry leaf serves as the surface of a bent-steel coffee table in the living room.	*A wood tabletop is supported by two bent steel plates.* *Translucent fabric suspended from wire tension cables diffuses natural light at the window wall.*	
Two planes of glass slipped at seven degrees cast diffuse light over the table.		
		The primary wood is cherry; however, planes of solid purpleheart are used for special elements such as the horizontal surfaces of the table and the vertical panels at the passageway between the living and dining spaces.
		The saturated, deep color of the purpleheart table provides an unusual backdrop for the occupant's collection of historic china, crystal, and silver.
		Fabric constructed for the project from natural and metallic fibers wraps the unexpectedly soft forms of the dining chairs.

materials

Existing surfaces of oak parquet flooring and plaster were restored to their original finishes. The herringbone floor pattern and ceiling-cove details indicate the 1920s provenance of the building.

New elements were constructed from a contrasting palette of materials. Steel and bronze were used for structural elements. Curly cherry and purpleheart were combined to create the perimeter storage wrapper. Planes of glass were layered to form translucent screens.

Bronze plate was folded to form lever door handles.

The active and passive
edges of the cabinet
doors illustrate the
relationship between
the two overlaid
geometries of the
space.

Black granite with cop-
per crystals furnishes a
durable surface for the
countertops and floor.

Bronze pulls, bent
from rectangular plate
at a seven-degree
alignment, create trape-
zoidal shapes. Pulls
are attached to obtuse
angled corners. The
adjacent corners are
sliced vertically to
avoid acute angled
corners, and to allow
a void space for a
finger pull.

Copper-and-glass-
mosaic tile provides
an animated reflective
backdrop at the work
surface. The small
grid offers a contrast
in scale with the
monolithic stone
counters and the
rhythm of wood panels.

Workplace for Publishing

oriented strand board
mineral strand board
birch
corrugated fiberglass
aluminum
aluminum dust
copper dust
granite

An office is a place where people accomplish common goals.

Publishing a new weekly magazine on arts and entertainment events in New York City requires a diverse group of energetic young culture consumers and an environment that supports creativity and communication. An open ten-thousand-square-foot loft space in Manhattan was the ideal container for the construction of an electronic village for a staff of seventy, including writers, critics, graphic designers, computer specialists, and support staff.

Villages develop around a central circulation axis and evolve in response to the available terrain, with occasional open spaces where the community can gather together. Similarly, this office plan evolved pragmatically along a street with clustered workstations forming small neighborhoods with their own shape and identity. Private offices and community spaces attach intermittently to existing window locations along the perimeter. Penetration of natural light is invited with the use of translucent partitions.

Several concepts explored in earlier projects initiated the design strategy:

translucence
planar elements
minimal transformation of materials
repetition

However, the constrained budget and schedule additionally suggested a solution that could go directly from building-supply shelf to installation. Two new concepts emerged:

stock materials
kit-of-parts assembly

By employing these concepts strategically, the project was designed and built within twelve weeks at a cost substantially below that of similar offices.

geometry

To emphasize the transitory nature of an office located in a building built at the turn of the century for manufacturing, the environment for the new use was disengaged from the clear orthogonal structure of the original space. The new architecture develops its own internal logic and geometry based on function and method of construction.

The basic planning module for the space is the individual workstation. Freestanding, clusterable, and assembled from a series of flat planes, the identical units serve both editorial and administrative staff. Clustered back-to-back or along walls, they provide raceways for data, voice, and power wiring and form the backbone of the office.

The central circulation axis offsets to either side of the line of existing cast-iron columns and bends to accommodate both new and existing functional areas. Clusters of workstations rotate and slip to avoid obstacles and maximize use of the available space.

Partitions for private offices, not constrained by orthogonal geometry, also rotate and slip to accommodate functional requirements and ease circulation.

structure

The interior street is defined by a series of translucent partitions that span vertically the space between the floor and ceiling and by an opposite series of free-standing solid screen walls cantilevered up from the floor, laterally braced by corner returns.

materials

New partitions and workstations were assembled from basic, off-the-shelf materials.

Translucent partitions of single-span corrugated fiberglass, largely self-supporting, were anchored and reinforced with light-gauge aluminum angles.

Solid partitions were constructed from oriented strand board on exposed wood-stud framing.

geometry **structure** **materials**

Oriented strand board is used to construct miscellaneous elements including a mail rack, reception desk, and solid partitions. The panels are assembled with simple detailing such as exposed edges and slotted construction.

A granite slab sits on top of the reception desk to provide a durable finish for a heavily used area.

Lightweight paper and wire lamps are suspended in special areas to provide localized incandescent lighting.

Cast-iron columns spaced equally down the centerline of the space become the counterpoint to the circulation axis, which weaves around them freely.

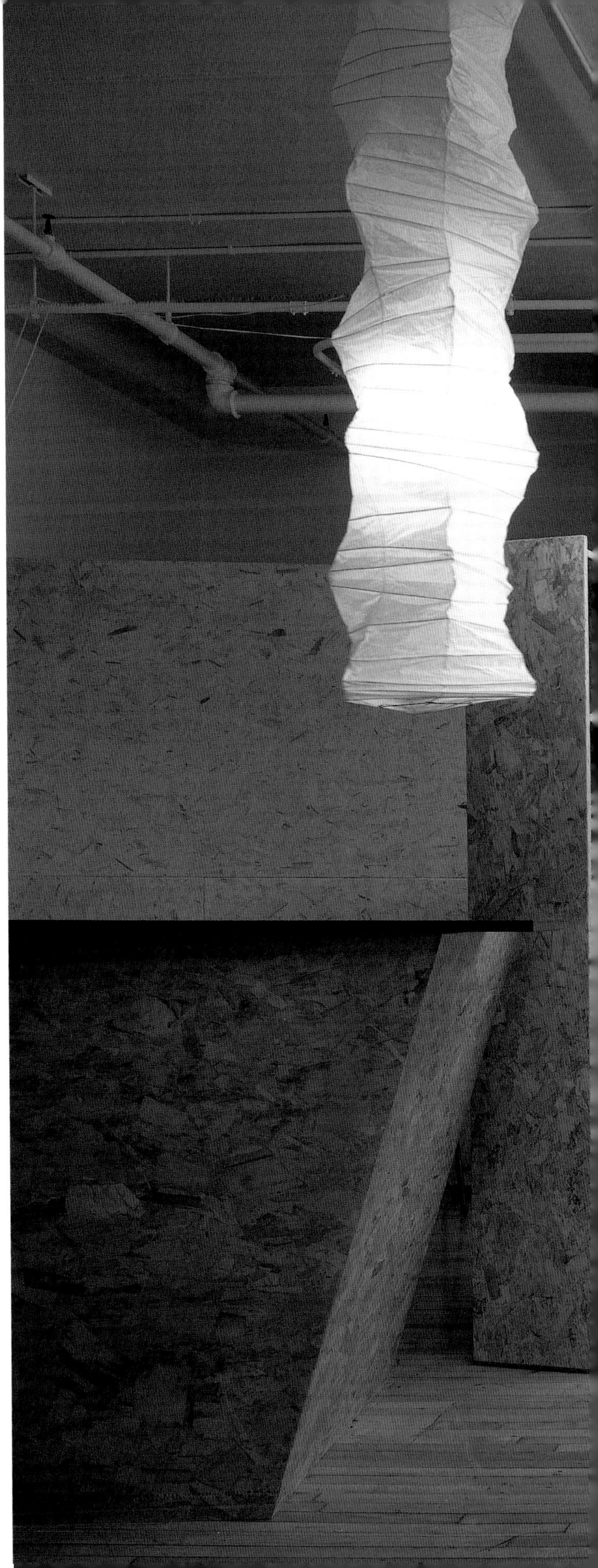

geometry	structure	materials

*The principal confer-
ence area is served by
a segmented table that
can be divided to create
two seating groups.*

*The regular rhythm of
exposed studs on the
screen wall establishes
an order in the space.*

*The table is an
assembly of horizontal
and vertical panels.
The bases are slotted
intersecting planes
that can easily be
disassembled. The tops
are self-supporting
cantilevers, balanced
on the bases and held
in place by gravity.*

*The table and screen
wall are both con-
structed of oriented
strand board, though
they are finished with
a subtle difference.
The screen wall, like
the workstations, has a
transparent white stain.
The tables throughout
the project are stained
with copper dust to
denote their more
elevated function.*

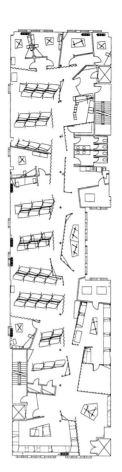
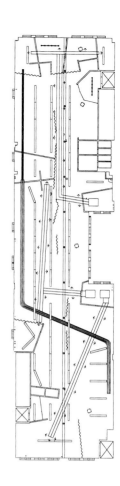

Repetition of vertical and horizontal planes of the workstations marks a rhythm in the space that reflects the scale of the individual person, the fundamental unit of the office community.

Workstations create a rhythm that is regular within each cluster but varies slightly from cluster to cluster, providing overall visual syncopation.

The simple form of the workstation, generated from planes and textures, provides a neutral backdrop for the individual identity of each staff member.

Taking full advantage of the standard dimension of the oriented strand board, the structural side panels project beyond the edges of the desks to create privacy and acoustic separation.

Horizontal surfaces at the desk and shelf are doubled to provide rigidity.

Lateral resistance for the fiberglass panels was achieved by overlapping panels at joints and reinforcing with a diagonal aluminum angle supporting both adjacent panels.

The integral textures of the materials create scale and contrast: the random figure in the oriented-strand-board workstations versus the linear pattern of the corrugated fiberglass and the random lengths of maple strip-flooring.

The light colors of all the finishes integrate the forms and textures.

geometry   structure

*The back panels of
the workstations span
horizontally and are
lifted off the floor,
providing closure for
the upper portion of
the workspace with a
single panel of stan-
dard four-foot-wide
material.*

*End panels are used
vertically as structural
columns as well as to
provide privacy
between workstations.*

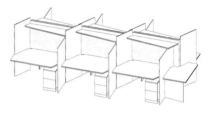

*The ganging of work-
stations creates an
offset order throughout
the space.*

*Triangular slots were
cut away from the
vertical panels of the
workstations to create
a horizontal wire chase
directly below desk
level. Workstation clus-
ters are fed horizontally
from central ceiling
drops with voice, data,
and power wiring,
leaving notches at
the end panels empty.*

geometry

To dematerialize the new construction, partitions and workstations were developed from thin planes and rotated within the space and from each other. The effects of light and space outweigh those of mass.

At the ceiling, cable conduits and ductwork follow an independent abstract geometry but are positioned to serve the new plan. Exposed ductwork is triangular folded sheet metal, forming one of the few volumetric elements in the space.

Lighting fixtures were deleted or rotated away from their original alignments to avoid conflict with the new construction.

materials

Crudely patched wood floors, cast-iron columns, and straight rows of industrial fluorescent light fixtures were inherited with the existing space.

Light is refracted through the fiberglass and shifts to create an unexpected pink glow.

Urban Park

1996

cobblestone
asphalt
concrete
glass
trees

An urban park is a respite from the city.

At the intersection of two street grids in Lower Manhattan, an underused one-way street and a small traffic island concealed behind parked cars provides the opportunity to create a large pedestrian precinct in a part of town with no major open spaces.

Using the bare minimum of means, the place is created from available elements:

limited removal of traffic
removal of parking
existing lighting
existing street trees
reconfiguration of pavement materials
fracturing and shifting the ground plane
penetration of the ground plane for light

In this proposal, the entire trapezoidal precinct becomes a huge urban sundial at the ground plane. Specific shadow patterns are projected onto the site from the rooflines of surrounding buildings at the moments of transition between each of the four seasons in the annual cycle:

autumnal equinox: September 21, 9:00 AM
winter solstice: December 21, 12:00 PM
vernal equinox: March 21, 3:00 PM
summer solstice: June 21, 6:00 PM

The pattern of these lines marks the shifts in the ground plane where the monolithic cobblestone surface of the park is fractured and shifted to create gently tilting planes. These planes rise and fall, creating seating for pedestrians along their edges. Existing street trees, now falling in an abstract pattern, provide a lacy canopy above.

One small segment of the surface is cut away to reveal the existing subway station and tracks. A glass prism is inserted in the void, glowing at night and refracting sunlight by day into this forgotten subterranean layer of the city below.

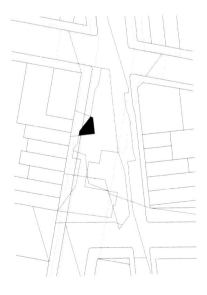

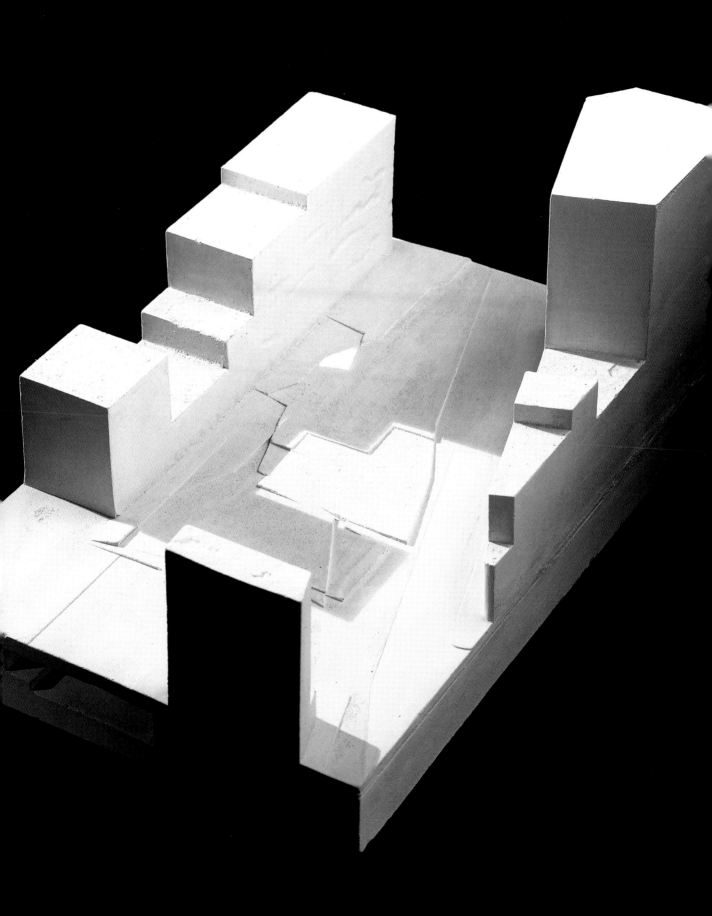

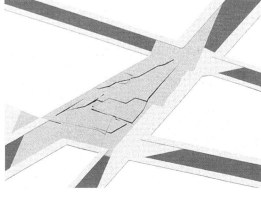

Cloister for Learning

gneiss
granite
slate
bluestone
shot-blasted steel plate
bronze plate
cherry
clear glass
dichroic glass

An academic building is a place for formal and informal intellectual exchange.

At a liberal arts college in Pennsylvania, the humanities departments had outgrown their facilities. The need for new space became an opportunity to shape the patterns of informal interaction between faculty and students that are fundamental to the learning experience at the school. In addition, the location and configuration of the building could be used to shape the outdoor spaces of the campus.

The new building represents a point on the evolutionary path of the college's Quaker heritage. Organizing principles of the existing campus fabric demanded respect:

axial planning
integration of landscape and architecture
primary building forms
multiple entrances
restrained detailing
native stone

Located centrally, straddling the historic axis, the building extends those traditional principles as it introduces concepts new to the campus:

balance of symmetry and asymmetry
figure/ground relationship of building and site
concept of building skin as wrapper
use of transparency to promote interaction
contrasting rhythms of fenestration
sensuality of surfaces

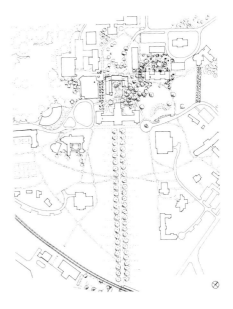

geometry

The rotated clock tower addresses the diagonal pedestrian circulation pattern of the north end of the campus. Its irregular facades stand in contrast to the rest of the building's regular rhythm of window openings and structural columns.

The geometric profile of the clock-tower roof joins an evolving campus tradition of towers, each signaling its period of architectural history.

The geometry of time is marked by a sundial embedded in the southwest face of the tower. Shadows from the gnomon are measured against hour lines, adjusted for the specific latitude and orientation of the wall. A special marker was inserted to indicate the one-hour shift from standard noon that occurs during daylight saving season.

structure

The steel-frame structure of the building is expressed by the regular rhythm of columns at the courtyard and by the articulation of the facade as a stone wrapper whose thickness is exposed at window slots and parapets.

Although the basic structure of the building is steel frame, the weight of the eight-inch-thick stone veneer is carried over window openings by a granite lintel.

materials

Walls are constructed of local gneiss, a sedimentary stone similar to granite. Following the tradition of the original humanities building, all surfaces are set in a random cobweb pattern except the more formal center bay, which exhibits a square-cut ashlar pattern. The ashlar pattern is used for the tower, as it is also a main entrance.

Rainbow granite from Minnesota is used for the dimension stone at window sills, lintels, and coping stones. It is also used for the two-inch-thick veneer panels of the column cladding as well as in other special areas where large surfaces are incised into the stone cladding, such as the tower entry and the window slot for the tower stair.

Dichroic glass laminated with various types of textured clear glass is used both for spandrel panels in glass slots and for translucent vision panels in adjacent areas.

The large gnomon, casting shadows onto the sundial, is a heavy bronze plate, cut and bent and anchored into the stone wall with triangulated bronze bolts.

The hour markers are black granite strips embedded into the ashlar stonework.

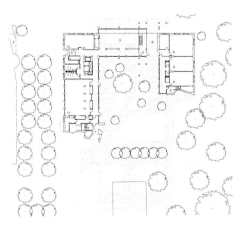

geometry

The ends of the two wings terminate the regular rhythm of the facades inside the courtyard with two different gestures: the tower emphasizes the vertical axis, while the shorter east wing emphasizes the horizontal.

A line of wood pylons marks the center axis of the campus as well as that of the new building. The pylons are used to display the arboretum's vine collection.

Window modules are multiples of the basic five-by-five-foot square used for the windows of the individual faculty offices.

Although the two upper floors of the wings follow the same plan, the windows are placed not at the center of each office but instead in a back-to-back pairing that results in the crenellated eave line. An effort was made to minimize the height of the eave in the courtyard area in order to allow maximum sun penetration and create an appealing and intimate outdoor space.

materials

During daylight hours, the dichroic glass panels reflect a soft or intensely colored light depending on the angle of incidence of the sun. At night, when backlit, the dichroic vision panels transmit subtle light of a different color.

Projected mortar joints in the new stonework match the joints of the original humanities building, giving continuity to the fabric of architectural materials on campus.

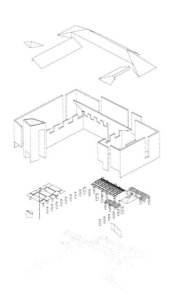

geometry

Repetition provides counterpoint to the cobweb stone pattern and syncopated rhythm of fenestration on the courtyard elevations. The solid granite trellis yields a pattern of parallel lines on each side of the passageway, as well as a related set of shadows on the adjacent stone surfaces.

The size and thickness of the granite column cladding is articulated in the pinwheel detail. This granite is not available in ten-foot lengths, so each column receives one six-foot and one four-foot set of panels. Their edges project beyond the corners in alternating directions and create a pattern emphasized by their shadows. To further develop the kinetic reading, the height of the panels alternates at every other column.

materials

Bluestone slabs set in an ashlar pattern continue in the courtyard, through the passageway, and into the building throughout the ground-floor public spaces.

The various joint patterns of the three types of stonework combine to create a geometric tapestry.

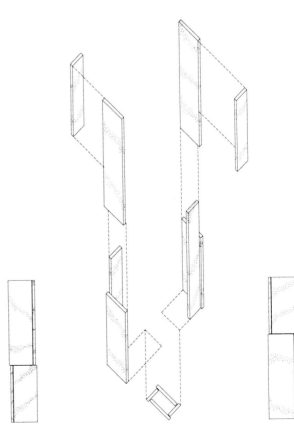

structure   materials

Edges and corners
provide opportunities
for expressing design
principles. The edges
of the panels of granite
veneer were exposed
to emphasize their role
in cladding rather than
load bearing.

The edge of the ashlar-
patterned center bay
overlaps the corner,
exposing its thickness
and therefore its iden-
tity as veneer. To
emphasize this condi-   Ashlar and cobweb
tion further, glass was   gneiss, granite, and
used for the adjacent   glass all come together
recessed wall.   at the corner of the
          formal principal facade.

geometry

*Many campus axes
align with elements
of the new building.
The centerline of the
new building follows
the central axis of the
original humanities
building and the formal
allée of trees that joins
it to the train station.
A passageway, offset
from the centerline
of the building, aligns
with one of the main
entrances of the origi-
nal building beyond.*

*The double-groin vault
over the passageway
marks the crossing
of circulation axes that
occurs below. The
longitudinal axis allows
pedestrians to cross
directly through the
courtyard, under the
building, and beyond
to the north side of
campus. The trans-
verse axis connects
the two halves of the
building together at
grade and provides
entrance to the class-
rooms in the east wing
or to the commons
and main stair in the
west wing.*

materials

*Glass-and-copper-
mosaic tile lines the
vault, reflecting light
both day and night.*

*The contrast between
the delicate shimmer
of glass tile and the
rough hand-hewn
texture of the rubble-
stone creates a memo-
rable experience in the
semicontained space.*

geometry

At the entry to the passageway from the north, many geometric elements of the project are combined: the series of trellis members standing on edge signals an important entry, and the vault ceiling beyond invites movement.

The window wall, with its staggered mullions and floating panels of dichroic glass, allows transparency into and out of the main stair day and night.

The large and small square windows represent the two sizes of individual windows used throughout the building.

The ashlar pattern of gneiss in the primary, central bay overlaps the cobweb walls of the balance of the building.

The thinness of the granite is expressed at the projected pinwheel corners of the column cladding while the integral thickness of the beam ends at the trellis is similarly exposed.

geometry

materials

Exterior materials also appear on the interior to create a sense of transparency and continuity at the ground floor.

Dichroic glass panels occurring in random locations, although in a repeating sequence of colors and textures, emphasize the paradox of glass: while it pretends to be invisible, it is as real as other materials. The panels express the materiality of the glass used in the horizontal window walls at the courtyard and elsewhere at ground level, and also at the vertical slots above the stairs and corridor ends.

The contrasting patterns and scales of the window mullions, cobweb gneiss, and bluestone paving frame views into the open public space beyond.

geometry

The seminar room at the top of the tower is trapezoidal in both plan and section, reflecting the non-orthogonal geometry of this part of the building.

A trapezoidal stone coffee table indicates the dual geometries of campus axis and tower rotation.

The forms of the custom-designed furniture also incorporate right-angle trapezoidal profiles.

materials

Frames for the chairs are solid cherry. They are upholstered with highly durable solution-dyed nylon that has been woven in a custom tapestry pattern.

The tabletop is made from granite for durability. The base is a bent steel plate.

The standing lamp consists of a granite base, a bent-steel-plate stem, and a bent-fiberglass shade.

geometry   structure   materials

Parallel rows of books
give order and identity
to faculty offices.

The sloping roofs at
the third floor facing
the courtyard create
unusual ceilings
for the offices below.

Cherry table-desks
with mobile pedestal
files allow the faculty
to work in an environ-
ment that feels domes-
tic, but the furniture
still accommodates
both a computer
workstation and a
traditional writing desk.

Relating to the desk,
solid-cherry trim with
a beveled edge is
attached to steel
system shelving.

geometry   structure   materials

Cherry veneer was used for the top, with a solid-cherry edge in two profiles. A narrow rectangular profile was used on the orthogonal edges. A wider, beveled profile was used for the non-orthogonal edges.

Solid-cherry chairs were used in the dedicated departmental seminar rooms to create an environment that feels domestic for these upper-class sessions, which traditionally were held in professors' homes.

Double trapezoid seminar tables allow maximum seating and maximum visibility for the departmental seminar rooms.

For the Sociology and Anthropology Department, special cherry cases have been provided for artifacts and theses.

Employing the maximum dimension of standard four-by-eight-foot material, the tabletops consist of four quadrants with one inside corner cut away to allow plugs for power or data connections to drop to the floor.

Bases constructed of intersecting wood panels create sturdy support for the table, which was built in two segments.

geometry   structure   materials

The solid-stone treads are supported on bent-steel stringers, which span between floors at the landings.

The bottom of both stairs and landings are exposed, revealing the pattern of the stone treads and panels at the landings.

Thermal-finish granite provides a durable, slip-resistant finish for the stair.

Solid-cherry handrails are warm to the touch and to the eye.

Dichroic glass was used for lighting diffusers on the wood-paneled wall, creating a play of soft colors and an interesting view at night from the exterior.

The solid-stone treads form trapezoids in section to create angled nosing.

Steel railings incorporate both orthogonal and non-orthogonal geometry. The balusters alternate between major vertical members and minor angled members, which are parallel to the angled front face of the treads.

Panels of cherry form a pattern on one side wall and incorporate recessed rectangular panels of lighting.

geometry   structure   materials

The five-bay space for this large meeting room is articulated with a checkerboard rhythm of two ceiling heights. The upper coffers are finished with a special acoustic plaster, contrasting with the smooth finish elsewhere. Indirect lighting was also used to emphasize this geometry.

Structural columns received a protective layer of wood paneling, unfolded at the top to reveal a light source.

Wood cladding at the columns received the same overlapping pinwheel detail at the corners as the granite column covers throughout the building.

Dichroic glass is used to create a translucent screen-wall at the exterior, continuing the full five-bay length of the room. Vision panels and ventilation are provided in the single casement window within each bay.

Dichroic glass was also used for the diffusers at the lighting in the wood column covers.

Center for Arts and Athletics

1997

concrete block
brick
copper
aluminum
glass

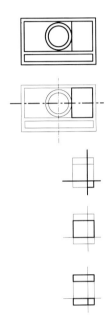

A community center gathers people of all ages and interests.

Occupying one end of an existing urban park in the Williamsburg neighborhood in Brooklyn, this community center combines space for athletics, club meetings, arts and crafts, and large neighborhood gatherings.

Several existing features of the site guided development of the site plan and diagram of the building:

> axial geometry
> existing path structure
> existing tree pattern

The building mass is organized into three blocks. One large wedge contains the large, multipurpose room and adjacent activity rooms; this mass is flanked by two secondary wedges that act like bookends, containing service and administrative functions.

A language evolved to connect the project elements visually:

> segmented forms
> floating planes
> sloping roofs
> transparency
> reversed wedges

The large glass wall of the multipurpose room and the strips of clerestory windows revealed by the stepping truss above provide generous views to the park and sky and become lanterns at night, marking the active life of this community facility.

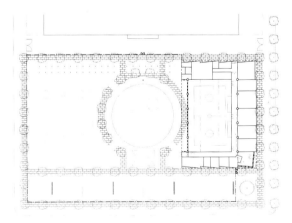

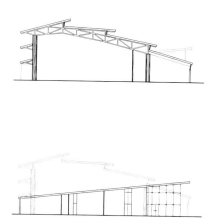

Temporary Workplace

parallel strand lumber
corrugated fiberglass
aluminum
vitreous steel
mineral strand board
pressed-fiber carpet

A temporary office accommodates demands of time and budget.

A new Internet advertising service provider in the Flatiron district of Manhattan met with such success that its staff grew exponentially in the second year. A temporary satellite location for the sales force would provide a short-term solution until plans could be made for a consolidated headquarters.

The space selected was divided into a rabbit warren of small rooms, an arrangement completely unsuited to the program. Accommodating nearly fifty people in a space smaller than five thousand square feet necessitated a high-density open plan. The program included a large bull pen for telephone sales as well as individual semiprivate workspaces for account executives. In addition, the space had to be designed and built at breakneck speed with a bare-bones budget. A strategic design approach was the only option:

> demolish all walls except service core
> do not disturb existing ceiling
> do not disturb existing lighting, ductwork, and sprinklers
> minimize general construction
> use off-the-shelf materials
> use panelized partitions in lieu of walls and doors
> build workstations off site as finished units
> design workstations to be transportable to next location

To reflect the energy and spirit of adventure of the young company, a bold palette of readily available inexpensive materials was employed. The materials provide economical and functional solutions to program requirements. At the same time they provide texture and animation in the somewhat ad hoc space. Each material serves a particular role; the unelaborated presence of each speaks visually.

geometry

To relieve the oppression and congestion of a highly dense orthogonal array, a slightly rotated grid is used for the shelves of the panelized workstations, the banding of two colors of carpet, and several partitions. This geometry is contrasted with the orthogonal grid of existing ceiling tiles and walls; the walls are cut off just below the ceiling plane and appear as suspended vestiges of an earlier time and use.

structure

All new partitions are constructed of rigid corrugated fiberglass supported by aluminum angle framing. Overlapping joints at the fiberglass panels are stiffened by angled secondary aluminum members.

The workstations are prefabricated as single units off site and either paired back-to-back or ganged in strips on site. Thick one-foot-wide planks of parallel strand lumber are used for overhead shelves or edge-laminated to create double-width vertical side panels or triple-width desktops. Structural back panels are made from medium-density fiberboard laminated on both sides to vitreous sheet-steel blackboard/tackboard. The structural design of the workstations follows the concept of a house of cards: triangulation is provided by the rotated overhead shelves. The desks are cantilevered from the side and back panels with one side given additional support by deep file cabinets.

Power and data wiring, encased in rigid metal tubing, is dropped from the ceiling to each workstation. The tubing passes down through a triangular opening formed by the rotation of the overhead shelf and, below, by a cutout in a corner of the desk. When workstations are ganged, the tubing travels horizontally through a triangular cutout below the desktop so that one vertical drop feeds multiple desks.

materials

Wood, the primary material, is used for the individual workstations, which represent the principal function in the space. The wood is an industrial by-product created from mill ends and second- and third-growth trees; it is typically used for top and bottom chords in truss joists where low cost and high structural capacity are key criteria.

The metal blackboard/tackboard panels are used for storing information at each workstation. Occupants use both chalk for making notes and magnets for tacking up printed information.

Pressed-fiber indoor-outdoor carpet is used in alternating bands of two neutral colors to create a sense of scale and individuality for each workstation in the open space.

Partitions, where required for privacy, are constructed of translucent fiberglass to allow light to penetrate.

Where ceilings are patched or infilled, a material different from the existing acoustic tile is used to emphasize the intervention. This material, tectum, is a mineral strand acoustical product with an interesting random linear squiggle pattern and deep texture.

geometry

The bull pen uses the typical workstations, which are ganged in parallel lines.

The functional logic of the plan is animated by the vestigial walls from the prior layout of the space, which are embedded into the ceiling overhead in a grid. Fluorescent light fixtures, air diffusers, and sprinklers also reflect the logic inherent in the previous plan.

The low shelves and backs of the workstations create a strong datum line in the space, above which heads are visible and active during the day as the sales fervor builds. Visibility across the room is essential to the work patterns, as is the white vitreous-steel scoreboard wrapping around the service core, where individuals' sales are posted daily.

materials

The stout materials and construction of the workstations stand up to the frenetic pace of their occupants. During the day the horizontal surfaces are piled deep with paper and files and the vertical magnetic blackboard|tackboard surfaces are covered with notes and memos.

The bands of the carpet, parallel with the overhead shelves of the workstations, create zones within the large space and differentiate the position of each desk.

The natural colors of the materials provide a calming backdrop for the pace and pitch of daily activities.

structure   **materials**

Semiprivate workspaces for account executives, arrayed in a straight line parallel to the exterior wall on one side and a fiberglass screen wall on the other, are created using minimal means. Privacy is achieved with high backs and overhead shelves that are well above eye level (when the occupants are seated). The rear partitions are created by the workstation behind. The vitreous-steel blackboards/tackboards on the rear surfaces create "walls" that are personalized by the occupants.

The pair of vertical drops for voice and data and power wiring at each station provides a vertical rhythm and anchors the workstations visually.

Materials are manipulated as little as possible; the goal was to achieve the required function with a minimum of elaboration and detailing. Fiberglass panels are used at their full eight-foot length. Aluminum angle is cut to length in the field from standard sizes. Parallel-strand-lumber panels are used in modular thicknesses and widths to create the workstations. Carpet is used in bands from typical twelve-foot-wide rolls. Recycled rubber tile is used in standard one-foot squares.

Workspace for Film Production

1998

sanded homosote
medium-density fiberboard
corrugated fiberglass
aluminum
cherry
bent steel
granite
recycled rubber
pressed-fiber carpet

An office for film production is a place for individual and collaborative work.

Conversion of a floor of a loft building on lower Fifth Avenue in Manhattan to create an office for a group of commercial film production companies involved several objectives:

> creating a dynamic but neutral backdrop for seven companies
> creating privacy and separation
> promoting cooperation and shared resources
> providing common meeting spaces
> maximizing penetration of natural light

The program called for a large number of private offices, guest offices, shared production and editing facilities, large meeting rooms to serve as team workrooms during planning sessions, and basic service spaces.

The need for many individual offices suggested a perimeter ring of private workspaces surrounding a central area containing circulation, informal seating, and meeting rooms. Similar to the residual open spaces between buildings that form piazzas in medieval villages, the central area is enlivened by its irregularity. At the same time necessary common functions are accommodated in a pragmatic way, further shaping these interstitial spaces.

The design solution followed a set of goals suggested by the program:

> demarcation of individual offices
> translucent perimeter partitions
> rotating walls in lieu of office doors
> sliding walls in lieu of conference-room doors

geometry

The irregularity of the existing floor plate is emphasized by the free plan, which oscillates between the orthogonal axes established by the structure and the diagonals of the rear wall and various new elements.

Alternating bands of carpet create a repetitive rhythm that is rotated from the structural grid. Flowing under all partitions, this order visually connects individual spaces to each other and to the collective whole.

Mechanical systems, voice and data wiring, and lighting are collected and distributed in a service soffit that circles above the perimeter offices and creates a consistent head condition for the translucent partitions and pivoting doors. The location of the soffit results from the alignments necessitated by its functions in individual spaces.

The staggered and overlapping configuration of fiberglass walls at the perimeter offices allows the doors to stand open during the day yet provides good visual privacy for their occupants.

structure

Partitions are constructed largely of modular materials for efficiency and economy. Corrugated fiberglass, cherry veneer plywood, medium-density fiberboard, and homosote, a recycled-wood-fiber product, are attached to light-gauge metal framing or, where framing is exposed, to aluminum angle. Exposed panel edges are slightly chamfered to ease alignment and express modular rhythms within the large vertical surfaces.

Oversize rolling walls at the conference rooms are field-constructed of two layers of cherry veneer plywood with staggered joints. They are suspended from rollers on an industrial track that is mounted to a steel channel at the beams above.

materials

Familiar materials are used in unfamiliar ways throughout the workplace. The transparent security enclosure at the elevator lobby is laminated glass mounted in laminated medium-density fiberboard framing. The reception desk is also fiberboard with granite slabs set on top to protect areas subjected to heavy use.

Perimeter office walls are translucent fiberglass to allow natural light from the exterior windows to penetrate.

The entrance door and office doors are pivoting planes of cherry plywood mounted to steel poles. This detail allows openings to read as mobile walls rather than as doors and thus maximizes the flow of space. In the open position, the doors reflect a warm glow through the fiberglass to the central space.

geometry   structure   materials

The diagonal alignment of the translucent office partitions mediates between the orthogonal orientation of the existing structure and the transient, ad hoc positions of the mobile pivoting doors.

The alternating bands of carpet provide a common reference throughout the space, visually connecting private and public spaces.

Desks are constructed from slabs of fiberboard edged with cherry planks. Support is provided by bent-steel-plate legs surface-fastened at the corners.

Cherry and fiberboard are used for surfaces that frequently come in contact with hands, such as doors, tabletops, and desktops.

Fiberboard is a cost-effective material for use as window-wall framing and baseboards as well as cabinets and desktops.

geometry   structure   materials

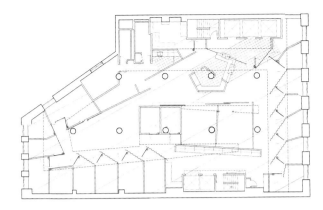

The existing load-bear-
ing masonry structure
is employed as a major
visual component of
the space. The discreet
detailing at the base
and capital of the
columns recalls the
history of the building
without looking out of
place in an interior
built a century later.
The grid of existing
beams above gives
scale and order to the
new plan.

Patterns are created
by the modules of
homosote wall cover-
ing, cherry veneer
plywood, and carpet.

The conference tables
are composed of slabs
of cherry veneer
plywood edged with
planks of solid cherry
and supported on bent
planes of cherry-veneer
plywood.

Homosote is used in
the conference rooms
as tackable, acoustically
absorbent paneling.
The surface is sanded
to create a sensual,
suedelike finish.

Project Teams

Garment Showroom
client — Jennifer Reed, Inc.
location — New York, New York
design team — Margaret Helfand, Paul Rosenblatt, Marti Cowan, Felecia Davis

Workspace for Architects
client — Margaret Helfand Architects
location — New York, New York
design team — Margaret Helfand, Marti Cowan

X, Y, Z, W Chairs
design team — Margaret Helfand, Marti Cowan

Apartment in Five Quadrants
client — Jay B. Adlersberg, M.D.
location — New York, New York
design team — Margaret Helfand, Marti Cowan, Felecia Davis

Industrial Building
client — Margaretville-Arkville Revitalization Project, Inc.
location — Arkville, New York
design team — Margaret Helfand, Marti Cowan

Art Museum
client — Rhode Island School of Design Museum of Art
location — Providence, Rhode Island
design team — Margaret Helfand, Marti Cowan

Apparel Shop
client — Buffalo, Inc.
location — Santa Monica, California
design team — Margaret Helfand, Marti Cowan, Monty Mitchell

Folded Corner Sconce
design team — Margaret Helfand, Marti Cowan

10 Vessels
design team — Margaret Helfand, Marti Cowan

Preassembled School
client — Bronx Community College Child Development Center, Inc.
location — Bronx, New York
design team — Margaret Helfand, Marti Cowan, Martin Zogran, Scott Mahaffey, Toby O'Rorke

Vertical House on a Trapezoidal Site
client — M. Lynne Markus and C. Donald Scales
location — Beverly Hills, California
design team — Margaret Helfand, Marti Cowan, Monty Mitchell

Segmented Table
design team — Margaret Helfand, Marti Cowan

Folded Handle
design team — Margaret Helfand, Marti Cowan

Apartment for Art and Music
client — Diane C. Bliss
location — New York, New York
design team — Margaret Helfand, Marti Cowan

Workplace for Publishing
client — Time Out New York Partners, LP
location — New York, New York
design team — Margaret Helfand, Marti Cowan, Martin Zogran, Meg Henry, Toby O'Rorke

Urban Park
client — Storefront for Art and Architecture and Lower Manhattan Cultural Council
location — New York, New York
design team — Margaret Helfand, John Tinmouth, Marti Cowan, Meg Henry, Jeff McKean

Cloister for Learning
client — Swarthmore College
location — Swarthmore, Pennsylvania
design team — Margaret Helfand, Marti Cowan, Martin Zogran, Toby O'Rorke, Scott Mahaffey, Meg Henry, Scott Carr, Brenda Barnes
with — Ehrenkrantz, Eckstut & Kuhn Architects, associated architect
Coe Lee Robinson Roesch, Inc., landscape consultant
Mary Miss, artist

Center for Arts and Athletics
client — New York City Housing Authority
location — Brooklyn, New York
design team — Margaret Helfand, Marti Cowan, John Tinmouth

Temporary Workplace
client — DoubleClick
location — New York, New York
design team — Margaret Helfand, Marti Cowan, John Tinmouth

Workspace for Film Production
client — Stoney Road Productions
location — New York, New York
design team — Margaret Helfand, Marti Cowan, John Tinmouth
with — Pugh + Scarpa, associated architect

special thanks to
Marti Cowan
an essential member of
the firm from 1986 to 1998

and to
Haggerty Woodworking
Mark Hill Fabrications, Inc.
Mechanic Street Pottery
& Ironworks
Peter J. Galdi Structural
Engineers
Pugh + Scarpa
Architecture/Engineering
Rudy Art Glass Studio
Taocon, Inc.